What people are s

Pagan Portals - Cerridwen

Pagan Portals - Cerridwen is a balanced approach to engaging with the well-known Welsh goddess, including both source material and a range of exercises for the reader to engage with, as well as an exploration of symbols associated with her including the cauldron. Short but packed with information this book is an excellent resource for anyone interested in Cerridwen or drawn to connect with her in witchcraft or pagan practice.
Morgan Daimler, author or *Pagan Portals - The Morrigan* & *Pagan Portals - Brigid*

Like the ingredients in the alchemical formula used by Cerridwen to create the Elixir of Wisdom, author, wisewoman, and Celticist Danu Forest deconstructs the story of Cerridwen into its component parts so that we may better understand the transformational nature of the whole. While doing so, Forest deftly weaves branches of folklore, legend, and history to create a coracle of cultural context that empowers the seeker to undertake a journey deep into the mysteries encoded in the deceptively simple tale of Taliesin. In addition to her excellent scholarship, Forest draws upon her decades of experience as a priestess, teacher, and practitioner to provide guided journey work that is centered in story, rooted in tradition, and potent in execution. *Cerridwen - Keeper of the Cauldron* is an excellent resource for anyone drawn to this Welsh Goddess of Inspiration – whether seeking to be in relationship with her for the first time, or deepening an already-established connection with her.
Jhenah Telyndru (MA, Celtic Studies), founder of the Sisterhood of Avalon, and author of *Pagan Portals - Rhiannon: Divine Queen of the Celtic Britons* and *Pagan Portals - Blodeuwedd: Welsh Goddess of Seasonal Sovereignty*

Danu Forest's *Cerridwen* is a skillfully woven book that is a perfect balance of sound scholarship and inspired personal gnosis, born of her years of academic study and lived experience as both priestess and wisewoman. Forest beautifully articulates each step of the tale of Taliesin, including corresponding experiential exercises artfully designed to deepen the reader's connection to the material on a transpersonal level. Highly recommended as both an in-depth introduction as well as for readers looking to expand their knowledge of this perennially fascinating subject in Welsh mythology.

Danielle Blackwood, author of *The Twelve Faces of the Goddess* and *A Lantern in the Dark*.

Forest has done it again! *Pagan Portals - Cerridwen* provides a wonderful introduction to one of the more revered figures in the pantheon of Welsh deities. At times enigmatic, and at others ferociously demanding, this book invites you into the story and along for the ride. Come and sit at the fire of Cerridwen on the banks of Llyn Tegid, meeting the other figures of that place. Stir her cauldron and dare to take a sip. Feel Cerridwen's wrath as her paws, beak and talons harass you in the chase. Cerridwen is a digestible experience that you will keep coming back to again and again.

Ben Stimpson, author of *Ancestral Whispers: A Guide to Developing Ancestor Veneration Practices*

Pagan Portals

Cerridwen

Keeper of the Cauldron

Pagan Portals
Cerridwen

Keeper of the Cauldron

Danu Forest

MOON
BOOKS
London, UK
Washington, DC, USA

CollectiveInk

First published by Moon Books, 2024
Moon Books is an imprint of Collective Ink Ltd.,
Unit 11, Shepperton House, 89 Shepperton Road, London, N1 3DF
office@collectiveinkbooks.com
www.collectiveinkbooks.com
www.moon-books.net

For distributor details and how to order please visit the 'Ordering' section on our website.

Text copyright: Danu Forest 2023

ISBN: 978 1 78904 188 0
978 1 78904 189 7 (ebook)
Library of Congress Control Number: 2023942947

A CIP catalogue record for this book is available from the British Library.

Design: Lapiz Digital Services

UK: Printed and bound by CPI Group (UK) Ltd, Croydon, CR0 4YY
Printed in North America by CPI GPS partners

We operate a distinctive and ethical publishing philosophy in all areas of our business, from our global network of authors to production and worldwide distribution.

Contents

Acknowledgments and Resources for Future Study

My interest in Taliesin and Cerridwen first took root within me while I was still at school over thirty years ago, and I remember how even then they stirred me deeply. The central work of this book has been to honour Cerridwen as best as I can, but no book, or journey of study ever takes place in a vacuum, and I would like to take this opportunity to thank and honour all those who have supported my path and learning, and who have provided insight and inspiration along the way. I would also like to acknowledge and honour the rich and vibrant culture and developments taking place with regards to this subject in modern Wales at this time, and to encourage the reader to engage with these as much as possible.

Firstly, I would like to thank my family for their unending support, especially Dan Goodfellow for his wonderful cover art. Copies of his Cerridwen painting can be purchased via www. dangoodfellow.co.uk. In addition, while their beliefs are not necessarily reflected in my work and any errors are my own, I would also like to thank my MA Celtic Studies tutors and PhD supervisors at the University of Wales Trinity St David and the Centre for Advanced Welsh and Celtic Studies, namely Dr Jane Cartwright, Dr Bettina Schmidt, Dr Ffion Jones and Dr Rhys Kaminsky-Jones for their impressive knowledge and insights. I'd also like to acknowledge the Welsh linguist Dr Simon Rodway, and Frank Oldings – again their beliefs and opinions are not necessarily reflected here but I want to thank them for their help with etymology and translation.

I would like to pay especial thanks and acknowledgment to the excellent Dr Gwilym Morus-Baird at https://celticsource. online. I have been fortunate to have joined several of his courses in the past and found them to be first rate and highly accessible.

I thank him also for his generous assistance over the years. Go check him out! As a native Welsh speaker and as an outstanding scholar and Taliesin specialist he must be acknowledged as a key voice in this arena.

I would also like to acknowledge the work of Kristoffer Hughes. Whilst I stuck to academic texts and my own insights and gnosis in response to my vision for this book, his book *Cerridwen - Celtic Goddess of Inspiration* is, of course, essential reading for those seeking spiritual connection with this Goddess. As a druid and native Welsh speaker his contribution to the native Welsh spiritual path is immense and invaluable. His other books are also highly recommended. Check him and the Anglesey Druid Order out at https://www.angleseydruidorder. co.uk. I have recently endorsed his latest book *The Book of Druidry: A Complete Introduction to the Magic & Wisdom of the Celtic Mysteries,* an expansive work which is essential reading for Welsh druidic study.

Continuing in my aim to highlight modern Welsh voices I would also like to acknowledge the excellent Swynwraig, author and folklorist Mhara Starling's contribution to the subject of Welsh myths and magic – you can find her on YouTube, Patreon and https://www.llewellyn.com/author.php?author_id=6824, and Sian Sibley of the Welsh Occult conference https://www. dragonoak.org. Also, the excellent work of Welsh folklorist Dr Delyth Badder https://www.folklorewales.com and Dr Jack Hunter's contribution to the area of visionary experience https:// jack-hunter.yourwebsitespace.com. Again, while the work of these individuals is exemplary, their inclusion here does not necessarily reflect their beliefs or opinions as much as my desire to highlight the wide scope and high quality of relevant spiritual and academic exploration within Welsh culture at this time and my encouragement of any readers of this book to discover for themselves the great work they have to offer.

Introduction

'Yr Awen a Ganaf, Or Dwfn y Dygaf'
I sing of the Awen, I draw it from the deep...[1]

Cerridwen is a goddess who is increasingly popular today. She is often thought of as a goddess of witches and magic, perhaps a mistress and initiatrix of life and death, and often she is portrayed as a 'crone' goddess, an old witch bent over her cauldron. But this is a modern vision of her, one which often overlooks Cerridwen as she is known in the traditional lore of her native Wales, where the vision of her is far more complex and nuanced.

The goddess Cerridwen, as we know her in the Welsh tradition, is a mother, fierce and predatory she none the less gives birth to her semi-divine son, the bardic magician Taliesin, and is deeply moved by her love for him, as well as by her love for her other children, Morfran and Creirwy. She is a fierce protectress, seeking to better the prospects of her son via her magical brew, the Awen. The face she shows us in her traditional lore, and perhaps even her name, may be one of many, her latest masks, and indeed what we know of her can only be seen through the lens of the medieval Christians that recorded her tale, leaving us with a sense of her mystery, but only tantalising glimpses rather than a clear and tidy narrative. She is not known of as a goddess in the remaining manuscripts that contain her tale, but rather a muse, at best, or at worst, a *gwrach*, a witch, a sorceress, which was no kind term in the days of her story being written down, unlike today. None the less, her power is so great, so enduring, that generation after generation are called to her side, drawn by her voice on the wind from the Otherworld, to partake of her brew and seek her magics anew.

1

In this book we will be looking at Cerridwen's surviving lore, mainly from her folktale, known as *Ystoria Taliesin* and *Hanes Taliesin*, which covers her initiation of the bardic magician Taliesin, and surrounding materials, which may shed light on the complexities of her most mysterious tradition. By exploring what was once known about this magical and formidable goddess, we may align ourselves more with her mysteries and deepen our connection with her, drawing on new and ancient threads of inspiration alike, and positioning ourselves within a continuum of practice potentially going back thousands of years. We also, then, aim to respect and honour the rich culture from which she is drawn, and may be fed from those deep roots, allowing us to bring in new insights, like leaves on a vast and ancient tree.

This small book is not meant to be a complete and conclusive study of Cerridwen – it could never be so as the subject is too vast and complex to fit in so few pages. Rather, it is intended as a grounded and researched introduction, one I write as a Celtic Studies academic but also as a practitioner and priestess of Cerridwen of many years, with research on one hand and my own gnosis on the other. Hopefully it may form a safe and steady place to stand, from which to explore your own connection to Cerridwen, to draw on her Awen in order to find inspiration and insights of your own.

May her brew be potent and bless you with every sip!

Endnote

1   Taliesin, 'Angar Kyfundawt', (The Malign Confederacy), translated by D. Forest, 2023. For an academic translation see Marged Haycock, *Legendary poems from the book of Taliesin*, CMCS, 2015. p119.

Part 1

The Quest for Vision

Cerridwen and the Awen

Any exploration of the goddess Cerridwen, and by extension her magical offspring Taliesin, cannot be undertaken without an understanding of the concept of *Awen*. In the Welsh bardic tradition, and in Celtic spiritual traditions generally, there is this concept – it's known as *Imbas* in the Irish. Inspiration and by extension, wisdom, are seen as an all-encompassing spiritual force, which imbues not only practical and magical knowledge but also the moral legitimacy of leaders and the ability to speak with the authority of the spirit world. It draws upon, or grants access to, the sum of human history and experience, as well as the knowledge of the cosmos, the stars and heavens, the gods, the dead and all spirits...in modern terms we may consider it to be akin to the collective unconscious. In the Welsh this is distilled down into the idea of poetic inspiration, in the bardic tradition, but this is not merely about rhyme and metre, it is about receiving the touch or breath of the divine, so that the poet or bard's words are drawn up and uttered from something beyond the human, from the very source of creation. Equally a leader such as a king or chieftain, or a soothsayer such as the

Welsh *awenyddion* used the Awen to express the will, or the voice, of the spirit world in order to apply its nourishment and wisdom in the mortal world. In this sense the bard is more akin to the prophet, or the shaman, speaking with the voice of the spirits or the gods. This thread of the Welsh bardic tradition is quite different to the praise poetry, used to honour kings and warriors (although the two are linked) in that while it is still intended for performance usually at court, it is deeply entwined with concepts of ritual theatre and magical ceremony. In this way we can see that the many mentions of Taliesin in the surviving texts can be understood as instances of his divine spirit being invoked via the bard's voice...so that he (or she) speaks with the voice of Taliesin, whose name means 'radiant browed' – or in other words, divinely 'illuminated'.

Taliesin, in his embodiment of the Awen, can be seen as a Welsh version of Buddha or Christ in this sense, although, of course, with different cultural and spiritual priorities and nuances. Indeed, it was widely believed that Taliesin had had many lives and was a spirit residing in Caer Sidi an aspect of the Brythonic Otherworld, Annwfn, when not in his physical form. As an initiate of Cerridwen's mysteries via his imbibing of her sacred brew, and his death and rebirth within her, Taliesin is a natural model for our own work with Cerridwen and our own quests for spiritual wisdom in her tradition.

The word *Awen* effectively means inspiration, and derives from the Indo-European root – *uel,* meaning 'to blow'. It is related to the Welsh word for breeze "awel" as well as the words for wind and gale in Cornish, which is part of the same stem of Celtic languages. Inspiration, from the Latin *inspirare* "blow into, breathe upon," figuratively "inspire, excite, inflame,"[1] has divine implications and was originally understood to be the breath of a god, used to give animation or life. This idea that breath and divinity are interlinked and life giving, is worldwide, and in the Bardic tradition it is seen as a means to draw wisdom and the voice of spirit or the muse into the bard's poems and performance, in a similar way to how prophets, mediums, or modern day channelers give voice to something beyond their personal experience.

The earliest attestation to the word *Awen* is found in Nennius[2] *Historia Brittonum*, (c. 796) drawn from the earlier works of the Welsh monk, Gildas. Nennius uses the phrase *'Tunc talhaern tat aguen in poemate claret'* (Talhaern the father of the muse was then renowned in poetry) referring to the poets of the 6th Century – aguen being the Old Welsh word for Awen as it is spelled today. We know that Awen was known as a source of instinctive or inner knowledge from its mentions in the 9th or 10th century collection of *Englynion* (short strictly metred poems), *Canu Llywarch Hen* where Llywarch says 'I know by my Awen'.[3] In turn, Awen is understood as being divine poetic inspiration from its numerous attestations in the 14th century Book of Taliesin (in Welsh – Llyfr Taliesin) which contains poems most probably from the 6th Century, which can be attested to the historical Taliesin himself. These earliest poems were most likely originally in the Cumbric dialect of Brittonic-speaking early medieval northern Britain, and became adapted and written down in the Brittonic Welsh at a later date.

Awen is often thought to be comprised of three aspects, or subdivisions (known as ogyrwen) and it was eventually given the symbol of 'the three rays', / I \ most probably by the 18th century antiquarian Iolo Morganwg. However, its tripartite nature is referred to repeatedly in the earlier bardic materials, as is its source within the cauldron of inspiration, or Cerridwen's cauldron. For example, there is this from the book of Taliesin;

ban pan doeth o peir
ogyrwen awen teir
"splendid was it when there emancipated from the cauldron, the ogyrwen of triune inspiration"[4]

The tripartite nature of the Awen is sometimes thought to relate to the Christian holy trinity, however, three has been seen as a sacred number since antiquity and is found throughout pre-Christian Celtic materials, from the triple aspected goddesses of Iron Age Celtic Europe to as far back as the triple spirals found on the neolithic tombs at the Boyne valley in Ireland and the sacred Brythonic triplicity of earth sea and sky. This triplicity, however, was one of several aspects of this tradition that made it easy to transpose these ideas into the emerging Christianity and would have been instrumental in its survival, albeit in an altered form.

Cerridwen is understood, in the Medieval bardic tradition, as being the divine muse or the embodiment of the Awen itself; sometimes she is described as being its mistress, overseeing and controlling its access and use. Some scholars will assert that this is where she belongs, and has no earlier presence or divine roots.[5] However, with other eyes it is possible and credible to see the traces of far earlier spiritual practices in the bardic tradition, which over the course of time survived and perhaps diminished in the Christian period from what was once an ecstatic, visionary cult where prophetic poets and warriors were initiated under the aegis of Cerridwen, known by this or another name, into a knowledge of the Otherworld and the realm of death from which they may return renewed and transformed.

Cerridwen and Taliesin

In Welsh mythology Cerridwen has long been known as an initiatory goddess, or enchantress, who over sees the pursuit of poetic wisdom and knowledge, understood as the *Awen,* or divine inspiration. What we know of her mostly comes from just a few medieval sources, largely the 14th century *Llyfr Taliesin,* or Book of Taliesin, a collection of poems attributed to the 6th Century poet Taliesin, where she is mentioned in passing, and the folkloric tale, *Ystoria Taliesin, Hanes Taliesin* or the *Story of*

Taliesin, dated in several written versions to the 16th and early 17th century, which are usually considered to be from far older oral sources.

Taliesin, whose name means 'radiant brow' is usually seen as the chief and most noble of the Welsh bards, historically and mythologically. It is likely there was an historical bard named Taliesin, going by that name, in the 6th century CE. Often known as *Taliesin Ben Beirdd* "Taliesin, Chief of Bards" or chief of poets, he is seen as the pinnacle of bardic ability, and it is likely other later poets called themselves Taliesin in an attempt to embody his semi-divine status, or to perform as if using his voice. He first appears in the surviving materials in Nennius's *Historia Brittonum* where he is mentioned as having lived in the time of Ida of Bernicia (mid-6th century CE.) and a British chieftain, Outigirn (Modern Welsh Eudeyrn, often Anglicised to Vortigern). The historical Taliesin was most likely a court poet composing praise songs in the court of King Urien Rheged (died circa 590). In contrast to this praise poetry, Taliesin is also credited as the author of the legendary poems, which are far stranger and more visionary in tone, lending an Otherworldly air in stark contrast with the praise poems of his courtly work. For this reason, it is commonly thought that there were at least two Taliesin's, the court bard, and this other stranger poet, who writes in a style well suited to oral transmission, and whose work is redolent of another earlier Wales, filled with spirits, magic and visions. It is this second Taliesin, filled with a strange and occult knowledge far beyond that of courtly rhyme and metre, who can be seen to be born of Cerridwen.

Taliesin the visionary poet is quite a different character than the courtly bard, he boasts of his vast age and seemingly endless knowledge, springing from his birth from Cerridwen. This Taliesin is magical; a shapeshifter, a magical defender, a recorder of the pursuits of mythical heroes and Otherworldly adventures, semi or fully divine, he is filled with light, the

Awen, or divine poetic inspiration, which flows from the brow of his head, illustrating his ever flowing inner spiritual or magical illumination. The tale of his birth, *Ystoria Taliesin*, has many things in common with the Irish tale of the boyhood of Fionn mac Cumhail and the salmon of wisdom – we will return to this later.

Endnotes

1 Inspiration, *Etymonline* https://www.etymonline.com/search?q=inspiration (accessed 06/23).

2 Nennius, *History of the Britons* (Historia Brittonum), (trans, J.A. Giles, Project Gutenberg, 1972) Kindle edition (Location 649).

3 Canu Llywarch Hen, stanza 55, (J. Koch, J. Carey, *The Celtic Heroic Age*. Celtic Studies Publications, Aberystwyth, 2003) p.390.

4 M. Haycock. 'Kadeir Teyrnon', *Legendary Poems from the Book of Taliesin* (CMCS, Aberystwyth,2007) p.296.

5 See R. Hutton, *The Pagan Religions of the Ancient British Isles: Their Nature and Legacy*, Blackwell Publishing, 1993, p. 323.

Part 2

The Tale of Cerridwen

Cerridwen and this mythological Taliesin are deeply intertwined in Welsh, or Brythonic lore, and it almost impossible to speak of Cerridwen without a deeper study of her poet offspring. We need to explore the tale of Taliesin, and his birth from the womb of Cerridwen, to discover the traces of earlier practices and how they reflect on what we can know about Cerridwen and her deeper mysteries. For this reason, we will now turn our attention to her tale as told in the *Ystoria Taliesin*, to hopefully unpick the threads of our surviving knowledge of her, and her functions in this strange and largely lost initiatory tradition.

A Brief Overview of the Texts

Llyfr Taliesin (The Book of Taliesin), one of the so-called 'Four Ancient Books of Wales', dates to the 14th Century and is one of our main sources for Cerridwen. It contains 60 poems, all dated to at least the 12th century, which were recorded by an unknown professional scribe drawn from earlier sources. It may have been complied before the existing poems were put together in this copy, and in some poems earlier language and spelling occur more frequently than in others, illustrating how the history of each poem's transmission is unlikely to have been uniform, with some being updated or recorded at different times than others. While other poems and folktales make mention of Taliesin, as well as Cerridwen, other than *Llyfr Taliesin*, the main source of our knowledge of her comes from the folktale, *Ystoria Taliesin* (the tale of Taliesin) and its alternative recording, the *Hanes Taliesin*, (the history of Taliesin.)

Parts or fragments of *Ystoria Taliesin*, in various amounts of completion, are found in some two dozen manuscripts written in Middle Welsh dating from the mid 1550's, drawn from oral sources which continued alongside the written tradition. The earliest source we have is a copy recorded by Roger Morris in the 16th century,[1] which in turn was copied by John Jones of Gellilyfdy around 1607[2]. This covers the early part of the tale with the boy Gwion being set to work for Cerridwen and his receiving of the Awen. Around the same period, around 1550, Elis Gruffydd recorded a version as part of his *Chronicle of the six ages of the world* which took the story further, into Taliesin's time with the lord Elphin at the court of Maelgwn Gwynedd.[3] John Jones made a copy of this manuscript around 1620, which in turn was copied by David Parry in 1698,[4] who titled it *Hanes Taliesin*. Parry added an additional section which has been lost in Gruffydd's version, making the story more complete. This version was recorded again by Evan Evans in 1765[5] and in turn by Iolo Morganwg in 1799.[6] Morgannwg's manuscript was in turn leant to Lady Charlotte Guest to be included in her translation of the collection of Welsh myths known as the *Mabinogi*.

We find our first mention of the bard Taliesin far earlier than any of these sources, as he is mentioned in Nennius's *Historia Brittonum*,[7] (9th Century), as one of five famed poets in the time of King Ida of Northumbria who lived in the 6th Century.

...then Talhaern the father of poetic inspiration (Awen) was renowned in poetry. And at the same time Aneirin, Taliesin, Bluchbardd and Cian who is called 'wheat of song' were famous in Welsh poetry.[8]

In this piece Taliesin is said to be the chief bard of Urien of Rheged, a kingdom covering much of Northern England, possibly as far south as Manchester, and into what is now southern Scotland as far north as Dumfries and Galloway. Urien is said to have been in power in the Dark Ages, not long after the fall of Rome and the end of British occupation, in the time of the mythical King Arthur, around the 5th and 6th century. We can therefore see that the figure of Taliesin, as a magical bard or enlightened initiate of the Awen dates to at least this period, possibly earlier, implying that Cerridwen, either by the same or another name, and certainly via her symbol the initiatory cauldron is likely to date, in some form, this far back also, and by extension into the pre-Christian Celtic period. Taliesin is also mentioned alongside Aneirin, with the figures Llywarch Hen and Myrddin (Merlin) in the Welsh rather than the Nennian Brythonic tradition, showing his influence extended over these two bardic strands of oral lore and positioning him both as a historical figure and a mythological one, as can be seen in the case of Myrddin / Merlin.

Cerridwen is also notably mentioned in the poems of *Prydydd y Moch*, (Poet of the Pigs) a bard from the late 12th century serving during the reigns of Dafydd ab Owain Gwynedd and Llywelyn ap Iorwerth, he was bard at the House of Aberffraw on the isle of Anglesey. Here he mentions Cerridwen, demonstrating the syncretism of both the pre-Christian and Christian traditions at the time.

"...the lord give me sweet awen, as from the cauldron of Cerridwen"[9]

In this way we can see that Cerridwen is associated with both the Awen and the cauldron from an early date, and across numerous locations in Wales and what is now northern England, and her connection with Taliesin was not exclusive, but merely her most famous initiated example.

The following is my own version of the tale, staying as true to the most recent translations as possible.

The Birth of Taliesin
This is the tale of Gwion Bach, widely known in Wales.

In the days of King Arthur, there was a lord of Bala Lake, in the area known now as Penllyn, and his name was Tegid Foel...the lake is named after him now, Llyn Tegid. He had a wife called Cerridwen, who it was said, was learned in the three arts of magic, enchantment and divination. She bore Tegid a son, who was said to be ugly, and have the hair of a red deer...people feared he was a demon, his name was Morfran, but people called him Afagddu, 'Pitch black, or utter darkness.'

His mother Cerridwen grieved for him and his looks and wanted him to be accepted and honoured among the people, so she thought that if she could give him great wisdom, and the gift of prophesy, he could win renown in that way instead. After long contemplation, she found a way through her arts, with the use of herbs, and hard work, and cunning... she gathered many special herbs, each at the right day and hour, and placed them in a great cauldron to boil. The cauldron was to be kept simmering for a year and a day, after which three drops would be produced, containing within them all the essence and virtue of the herbs. Whoever took those three drops within them would then be expert in various arts and filled to the brim with the very spirit of prophecy. Once taken, the rest of the brew within the cauldron would become the most powerful poison in the world which would burst the cauldron and spill out across the land.

Cerridwen gathered the herbs, and put them in her cauldron, and this she placed over a fire. She had an old man, Morda, and a young boy, Gwion Bach to keep the fire going and to stir the potion. And so, the old man and the boy kept to their work, stirring the brew and tending the fire, while Cerridwen kept adding the herbs and the water, until the year and a day had passed.

At the due time, Cerridwen took her son Morfran to the cauldrons edge, to receive the three drops when they sprung forth, and then she lay down to rest, and was soon deep asleep. When suddenly, up sprang the drops out of the cauldron, yet it was Gwion who had them! For he had pushed Morfran out of the way at the last moment. Immediately the cauldron cracked, and the poison spilled forth, and Cerridwen woke with a start, and no sooner was she awake than she saw Gwion and was like a madwoman in her frenzy. Gwion, however, was now full of the knowledge from the cauldron, and could see for himself that she would kill him, so he ran. Cerridwen gathered her senses, and asked Morfran what had happened, and he told her how Gwion had pushed him out of the way, and so she ran after him, in swift pursuit. As the story says, she saw him running, as fast as he could, in the shape of a hare, and so she turned herself into a greyhound, all the better to chase him from place to place. Then he reached the river, and turned himself into a fish, but she turned herself into an otter, to catch him all the easier. Then he took to the air as a bird, but Cerridwen turned herself into a hawk from which he could not escape...so he turned himself into a single grain of wheat, and still Cerridwen pursued him. She turned herself into a black hen, scratching at the floor or the barn, and in that form, she swallowed him whole.

Cerridwen carried the grain of wheat within her for nine whole months, where he grew in her womb into a beautiful boy, after which she gave birth to him.

And when she saw this beautiful boy in her arms, she knew she could do him no harm, nor allow any harm to ever come to him. And so she placed him into a coracle, or some say, a leather bag, and she wrapped him tight and warm, and cast him out onto the lake, or as some say, afloat upon the river, and out to sea, for forty years.

He is found at last, having finally drifted to the shore, by Elphin, the son of the king Gwyddno Garanhir, Lord of Ceredigion, who was down on his luck. Taliesin was still in the form of an infant, lying within his coracle, when Elphin found him while fishing for salmon, long a symbol of wisdom. Elphin found no salmon but instead finds Taliesin's coracle. He reached within, and uncovered the baby, and was immediately struck by the boy's beauty and the light emanating from him. Elphin named him then, calling him *Taliesin* meaning *'radiant brow'* as a description of his beauty and inner illumination. This infant Taliesin is, however, no ordinary child, and is already exclaiming the most incredible poetry, and displaying divine wisdom and magical ability. Elffin brings the young boy back to court with him, and Taliesin quickly overturns Elffin's fortunes as well as immediately becoming the chief of all bards...reducing the other bards at court to fools as he enchants them so that they can only mutter the baby noises *'blwrm blwrm...'* In comparison to his eloquence and wisdom.

Working Through the Tale

To explore the depths of this tale, and discover more about Cerridwen, we need to look through the tale above step by step and uncover its layers of meaning. Some of these are literal and logical, while others are felt and more experiential in nature, leading us into an ever-deepening understanding.

Cerridwen

Cerridwen as a name is given to several interpretations, just as her figure is seen in different ways. The earliest written version of her name is *Cyrridven*, which occurs in the Black Book of Carmarthen (13th century). The noted Welsh Scholar Sir Ifor Williams, translates this name as "crooked woman",[10] although the stems *cyrrid* and *cwrr* (sometimes translated as "crooked" or "hooked" from the Old Welsh cwrr – corner) are debated and unclear. Ben/ven means "woman" or "female" in Welsh, and Williams' translation presumes that the 'Wen' in Cerridwen refers to her being a 'crooked woman' – meaning a hag, suggesting a witch bent over her cauldron, or perhaps crooked as in tricky or deceiving. It may be a term that is consciously misogynistic, given to the goddess by Medieval clerics, equally it also be a poetic term for the crescent moon as the moon is often considered to be female. Either way, its likely that her tale is a cultural memory of a mystery tradition that was sadly fading or even long gone by the Middle Ages but of such importance that it survived the transition into Christianity, if only in memory.

Further interpretations of her name come from the eminent Welsh scholar, Marged Haycock, who suggests *cwrr-rhit-ben* 'woman with angular embrace', which seems hard to explain. In addition, Haycock suggests that the *Cerrid* part may be drawn from *cryd* 'fever, ague, shakes'[11] which is interesting when we consider her to be the creator of a mystical visionary brew – was such a brew ever made by the early Welsh bards and their predecessors? People taking modern entheogenic brews today such as Ayahuasca may tremble, have temperature variations and even be sick as part of the visionary process and its effects upon the body. Similarly, the Welsh Awenyddion, (soothsayers) recorded at the end of the 12th century, appeared to shake when in trance like states, during which they sought answers from the spirit world.[12] Haycock also suggests another option, that *Cerrid* is from *Creit,* (passionate, inflamed woman)[13] which could infer being lit with the flame of inspiration, or again having a high temperature due to intoxicants. A final possibility that Haycock offers is *cred* – 'believes', or 'to be believed in' which is also attested in the word *creir,* which is probably the first element in the name of Cerridwen's daughter Creirwy, making them a pair.[14]

To summarise then, Cerridwen may mean 'crooked woman' referring to her being an old woman, perhaps associated with witchcraft and the crescent moon, and this has some validity but it has one major problem. Cerridwen is not an old woman, she is clearly of childbearing years, the mother of three children, one a baby, by the end of the tale. Haycock's interpretation that she may be a fevered or shaking woman is definitely suggestive of some kind of visionary frenzy and I feel this argument has great weight, as is the idea from *Cred* that her name implies, she is a figure to be believed in, and that there is a partnership or relationship between that and the name of her daughter Creirwy. That the meaning Cyrrid or Cerrid is still debated shows how much we have lost of this lore over time, and again suggests the antiquity of the tale and its transition into the Christian era and the written form. A tempting interpretation of the word Cyrrid, bent or crooked, from the word for corner, is to see is as suggesting something that turns, like the spiral stirring of the cauldron and the wheel of time. A wisdom or magic that is in itself ever moving and changing much as the shapeshifter herself. Considering all the scholarly linguistic options carefully I find I want to allow the Awen the final say, however, and personally take a rather poetic approach to the translation of her name, allowing my inner vision to consider her 'The seeress of the inner flame.' A woman who shakes and is fevered with visions that you can believe in.

Cerridwen and the Fferyllt

While Cerridwen is noted as skilled in sorcery and in the Elis Gruffydd version of the tale, she is said to be learned in three arts, magic, enchantment, and divination. Cerridwen is said to have been consulting the *'books of the Fferyllt'* to boil the cauldron. Fferyllt in Welsh usually means alchemist or magician, and is in fact derived from the Welsh name for the Roman poet Virgil. It is this alchemical knowledge and skill that is to be used to transform Morfran. In this context the transformative journey which Gwion undertakes by imbibing the brew from the cauldron can be seen as a process of turning the base matter of Morfran's 'utter darkness' into the gold or illumination of Taliesin. To use the term Fferyllt places Cerridwen's magic firmly in the 'high magic' traditions of medieval Europe, something the Welsh courts at the time of the tales recording into manuscript form would be well acquainted with. It is likely that the inclusion of the term Fferyllt is a later medieval addition to the tale to further elucidate what is occurring, but in doing so an older, more native tradition is being obscured, one which would have until that time been retained in the oral versions of the tale. In the same way, the character of Cerridwen is also obscured perhaps, from initiatrix and keeper of the Welsh oracular mysteries, into the furious witch seeking vengeance performing distinctly European magic instead of the older Druidry of her native land.

Exercise: Meeting Cerridwen

In this exercise, we will seek to encounter Cerridwen, and make some first steps into connecting with her and receiving her tuition, in the inner realms of Annwn. For some, this may be a deep and profound thing, for others it may be a meditation on what we know about her and what we can glean from the surviving evidence of her veneration. Let it unfold as it will, as a first step, or as a deepening experience allowing her presence, and the Awen, to reveal what it will for you at this time.

Give yourself 20 minutes uninterrupted time for this exercise. Create a safe and comfortable sacred space, in which ever way you prefer, and light a central candle in honour of Cerridwen.

Take three deep breaths for water, three for air and three for land, and close your eyes or let your vision rest gently upon the candle flame.

Let your awareness soften and the room around you fade away. In your inner vision focus your mind upon a simple scene, of a woman standing alone by a lakeside. Let your breath carry you deeper into the scene, and ask that you may be granted an audience with Cerridwen at this time, to deepen your knowledge of her and give her your respects.

The air around you is cool but not cold, and the day is turning to evening, with the sky a soft deep blue, with the first scattering of stars beginning to come out. The lake before you is still and quiet, gently lapping at the shore, as you find yourself approaching the woman, who stands a few feet away from some oak trees, their roots risen up and exposed upon the earth like twisted limbs. She stands tall and silent, her feet in the water.

As you approach, she turns and looks deep into your eyes, before silently heading off between the trees to where there is a fire, newly kindled, with a tripod and a cauldron, hanging above it.

She stands, with the lake on one side and the cauldron on the other. Greet her in your own words, and offer her your respect. Depending on how she responds, you may ask her questions which she may or may not answer, but if you are clear in your intention to learn from her at this sacred place, and to glean the wisdom from her tale, announce this to her and ask her permission, that she may bless your work and guide you into gaining the insight and illumination that you seek.

Let your time here unfold as it will, perhaps asking about the lake, the fire, and the cauldron, and its contents... pay attention not only how she appears to you, her age and bearing, but also to how it feels to be here. Pay particular attention to any shifting sensations or changes of consciousness or new insights you may experience now or later.

When the time is right, Cerridwen will dismiss you. Give her your gratitude and return the way you came through the trees, letting your breath carry you. Let the vision fade, and your spirit return to the room in which your body sits. Wiggle your toes and shake out your arms and hands to feel yourself back into your body. Close your sacred space and extinguish your candle, thanking Cerridwen for her tuition. Take some time to eat and drink to fully ground yourself back in the present, and record your experiences in your journal if you wish.

Cerridwen and Fire/Cauldron

Tegid Foel

Tegid Foel – meaning beautiful the bald, is the name of Cerridwen's husband, who gives his name to Llyn Tegid, now also known as Bala Lake. Sometimes Tegid Foel is thought to be a version of the name Tacitus – after the Roman historian Tacitus, who wrote about Wales, marking Rome's presence in the area. However, Tegid Foel is also commonly thought of as the giant of Pennllyn (an area around Bala) – his identity as a giant makes it more likely that he was considered a divinity at some point, perhaps a genius loci or local god of the area.

The lake associated with Tegid Foel, Llyn Tegid, is the largest natural body of water in Wales, and is renowned for its beauty, and the clarity of its water. Located in the county of Gwynedd, North West Wales, local legend has it that the court of Tegid Foel was eventually drowned, perhaps at the breaking of the Cauldron, and now lies beneath the waters...and on bright moonlit nights it can be seen far below. Another tale tells of how a sacred well was visited by the devil and overflowed drowning his kingdom and forming the lake.

The location of Tegid's court and its drowning is interesting especially as in the life of Taliesin, Taliesin's patron Elphin is the son of the lord Gwyddno Garanhir, who's kingdom Cantre'r Gwaelod (English: the lowland hundred) was also eventually drowned, and is said in folklore to lie somewhere between Ramsey Island and Bardsey Island, under what is now the relatively shallow waters of Cardigan Bay. Cantre'r Gwaelod was said to have been drowned when a woman, Mererid, neglected her duties and let the well overflow, a tale that mirrors again in some way that of the cauldron cracking and overflowing in Cerridwen's tale.

Exercise: Meeting Tegid Foel
In this exercise we will be spending some time meditating on and perhaps meeting with Tegid Foel. Just as before, how deep this

experience will be will depend very much on the individual. See this as a first step and an opportunity to meditate on the tale and those involved, and seek contact on the inner realms of Annwn, where possible.

Give yourself 20 minutes uninterrupted time for this exercise. Create a safe and comfortable sacred space, in which ever way you prefer, and light a central candle in honour of Cerridwen, as described earlier.

Take three deep breaths for water, three for air and three for land, and close your eyes or let your vision rest gently upon the candle flame, asserting your intention this time, to meet the Otherworld king, Tegid Foel.

Let your awareness soften and the room around you fade away and see yourself walking slowly towards the lake. Again, the sky is a deepening blue of early evening, with the first stars coming out, reflected in the gentle surface of the water.

Bow your head and ask to receive and audience with the lord of the lake, and then let your eyes rest upon the water.

After a time, a figure approaches, and as he grows nearer you see he is a large man, seemingly walking across the surface of the lake. He wears a cloak the same colour as the water and the sky.

What will you say to him? What will you ask him of the significance of this tale, and of the lake itself? Perhaps if he is willing, he will take you to his castle beneath the waters, or show you the mysteries of the lake itself.

Let your time here unfold as it will, focus on building a relationship and on allowing space to receive whatever communication he offers you, in whatever form that takes.

After a while the meeting will naturally come to a conclusion. Give him your thanks, and return the way you came through the trees. Letting your breath carry you, let the vision fade, and your spirit return to the room in which your body sits. Wiggle your toes and shake out your arms and hands to feel yourself back into your body. Close your sacred space and extinguish your candle, thanking

Cerridwen for her tuition. Take some time to eat and drink to fully ground yourself back in the present, and record your experiences in your journal if you wish.

Morfran Afagddu

Cerridwen's son, Morfran, whose name means 'the great crow' or alternatively, 'sea raven' is an interesting feature of the tale. Crows and ravens are always significant in both Brythonic and Gaelic mythology, and are often associated with lore and knowledge as well as war, death, and destruction, the chthonic forces of creation. In Welsh myth the god/ king Brân the blessed is seen as a giant, and a great guardian of the land. His name Brân means crow or raven, and his sister, Branwen, or white crow is caught in between a great conflict between the Welsh and the Irish. In her tale she dies of a broken heart as a result of the disastrous raid upon Ireland to rescue her, which resulted in mass death apart from only seven heroes. Etymologically, it is likely the Brân/ Branwen were originally one war goddess, linking her perhaps to the Irish figure of the Morrigan.

That Cerridwen sees her son Morfran as being in need of great wisdom, so that he would have renown and be held in honour by gentle folk, points perhaps to him as some kind of destructive force, or embodying some kind of chthonic quality, that is in need of evolving into a more sophisticated form. His 'ugliness' does not seem matched, however, with any particular aggression, as in Gruffydd's version of the tale (*Ystoria Taliesin*) he is easily pushed aside from the cauldron by the boy Gwion. Instead, he seems to be a guileless and unassertive individual that is in need of extra care from his mother. Later in his life, however, it is recorded in the myths that he appears in the battle of Camlan, where he is one of the few survivors, due to the terror other warriors feel at his appearance. It is said he has the hair of a red deer, suggesting he is animalistic in some way, perhaps hinting at some kind of shamanic or animistic transformation, or linking him with the earlier Celtic gods such as Cernunnos, who is depicted with horns and antlers and associated with deer. Hunter gods are a common feature in pre-Christian religions all around the world, associated with the wild and untamed aspects of nature, as well as fertility, hunting and culling – bringing death when it is due to maintain a cosmic or environmental balance.

Cernunnos appears most famously on the beautiful Gundestrup cauldron, whose features amongst his cult animals of snakes and stags, and whose panel is positioned amongst others clearly depicting warriors being placed inside cast cauldron by a goddess – distinguished by her giant size compared to the men she submerges within the depths of her sacred vessel. In some ways the images upon the Gundestrup cauldron may be presenting another version of the Taliesin tale, with the subversion of men into the cauldron for transformation, death and rebirth.

Morfran is said to have been given the name Afagddu, whose name has no agreed translation, but is commonly thought to mean 'pitch darkness', ('y fagddu' in modern Welsh), due to his ugliness, while in some versions, Afagddu is Cerridwen's second son. Yet the notions of the great crow, and 'pitch darkness' are closely intertwined as symbols of destructive force, death and decay, and perhaps the alchemical idea of 'base matter' unevolved material which can by alchemical transformation, become enlightened, just as Gwion becomes when he is reborn as Taliesin. Haycock states that *Afag* – could be a borrowing of Irish *abac* 'dwarf, leprechaun', which in turn is cognate with Welsh afanc 'water-monster' which adds additional ideas about his role or appearance, as a monstrous, Otherworldly being.[14] Indeed, there is a local legend at Bala that an afanc, or water monster dwells in the lake, connecting local knowledge with this story once again.

There is another aspect to consider when we look at Afagddu and his darkness – that he may be such a powerful Otherworldly presence that he is obscured in some way from the eyes of the mortal word. Other mentions of him in the lore suggest that he did indeed gain the Awen at some point, and that his poems are too dense and obscure to be fully understood by the living, suggesting his wisdom and visionary prowess are advanced indeed. For example, he is mentioned in the poem *Angar Kyfundawt* (The hostile alliance) alongside Taliesin, Cian and Gwiawn as a bard of renown...*'By lleith bit (ardu), arieth Auacdu'* (Until death it shall be obscure, Afagddu's declamation).[15] In this way Afagddu / Morfran may be seen as a bard of the Otherworld rather than the mortal realm.

Exercise: Meeting Morfran / Afagddu

In this exercise, just as before, we will be spending some time considering Morfran, and perhaps meeting him in our inner vision. As always how deeply you will experience this is dependent on your own personal development and ability, but each time you will find you gain deeper and deeper insight.

Give yourself 20 minutes uninterrupted time for this exercise. Create a safe and comfortable sacred space, in which ever why you prefer, and again light a central candle for in honour of Cerridwen.

Take three deep breaths for water, three for air and three for land, and close your eyes or let your vision rest gently upon the candle flame.

Let your awareness soften and the room around you fade away, and in your inner vision focus your mind upon a simple scene, of a young man standing beside the lake, silhouetted against the still pale blue of the water and sky. As you walk towards him you become aware of his reflection stretching out long and dark in the water. Listen to your gut here, how does it feel to approach this figure? Greet him quietly, with respect, and see how he responds. Stand by the waters edge and look at your own reflection, next to his. Do you share anything in common?

Take your time here, let the journey unfold as it will, together with your conversation. You may like to ask Morfran about how he sees the world, and about his name. Ask him if he knows about Afagddu... this sacred being has much to teach us about transformation, and how appearances may differ from someone's true nature, and about compassion for our shadow selves. Most of all, seek to listen to this being, and pay heed to your inner promptings.

Let your time here unfold as it will, focus on building a relationship and on allowing space to receive whatever communication he offers you, in whatever form that takes.

After a while the meeting will naturally come to a conclusion. Give him your thanks, and return the way you came. Letting your breath carry you, let the vision fade, and your spirit return to the room in which your body sits. Wiggle your toes and shake out your arms and hands to feel yourself back into your body. Close your sacred space and extinguish your candle, thanking Cerridwen for her tuition. Take some time to eat and drink to fully ground yourself back in the present, and record your experiences in your journal if you wish.

Creirwy

Cerridwen's daughter, Creirwy is only mentioned in the John Jones *Hanes Taliesin* versions of the tale, and in the Welsh Triads. By contrast to her brother Morfran, she is described in the *Hanes Taliesin* as 'the fairest maid in the Isle of Britain'[16] and her name appears to be drawn from the Welsh word for relic or other sacred item or treasure – 'crair'. Jones calls Cerridwen's daughter Greirfyw / Creirfyw, which is formed from *Crair*, (treasure, heirloom, precious or sacred possession) from the root Cred (to be believed in) and *Byw* (living, lively) giving the meaning "lively treasure", "living treasure". The *wy* part of Creirwy is a common suffix in Welsh names and place names. In place names it suggests 'the place of...' or 'the land of...', but in personal names it works as an intensifier so in the case of Creirwy it suggests 'Very precious treasure' or 'very lively precious treasure'. The linguist, Ifor Williams, gives her name as 'lively darling'.[17] Haycock connects Cerridwen to Creirwy as names via *Crair / cred-* 'to be believed in'[18] making her 'the very treasured one' – perhaps implying she is the product or treasured goal when seeking Cerridwen's mantic vision, or the result of being inflamed via her entheogenic brew.

There was a 6th century Breton saint by the name of Creirwy, whose tale tells us she originated in Wales. She was the sister of St. Winwaloe, and had her eyes plucked out by a goose but had her sight restored[19] and became the patron saint of the blind – and intriguing aside to a tale concerning the gaining of inner vision which is a continual thread through Creirwy's tale.

As Cerridwen's daughter it may be possible to see Creirwy as the Awen itself, or as earlier generations of Celticists asserted, that she may indeed be another name for Cerridwen who can also be understood as the embodiment of Awen. If we assume that her name means 'lively precious treasure' then a connection to the Awen becomes overt – a treasure that is 'lively' that grows and moves, is not a fixed or static thing. A living treasure that moves and flows is not a physical treasure – it is energy, and knowledge, inspiration, the breath of spirit, the very Awen itself that is ever changing and still the very greatest treasure of them all.

The influential 19th Century Celticist, Edward Davies, was of the opinion the Creirwy was "the Proserpine of the British Druids"[20] equating Cerridwen with the Roman goddess Ceres, likening them both to the tale of Demeter and Persephone, as the goddess of the grain and crops and her daughters recurring journey to the underworld in the winter months. In this context we would see the cauldron again be an access point to the underworld or realm of the dead although in *Hanes Taliesin* we see no mention of Creirwy descending within it or imbibing its brew. The Classical allusions found in *Hanes Taliesin* clearly suggest the story was at the time of writing being told with these mysteries in mind and perhaps an attempt to equate native Welsh lore with that of the Greeks and Romans. However, even if that were the case these motifs concerning the descent into the underworld and the rise anew are found all over the world in oral tales as well as finding their natural echo in the human condition.

Edward Davies also asserts that Creirwy shares further links with the tale of Brân and Branwen, as like Branwen 'White crow' she has a brother who is the dark crow or raven, and both are associated with a transformational cauldron. Links can also be seen when we consider Creirwy as a Persephone figure, with the story of Gwyn ap Nudd the lord of the Welsh / Brythonic underworld Annwn and his abduction of Creiddylad. Certainly, the parallels are there to be seen, hinting yet again at a now half-forgotten mystery tradition that it is possible to sense when we look at the material but impossible to prove with any detail or certainty.

Exercise: Meeting Creirwy

In this exercise we will be spending some time meditating on and perhaps meeting with Creirwy. Just as before, how deep this experience will be will depend very much on the individual. See this as a first step and an opportunity to meditate on the tale and those involved, and seek contact on the inner realms of Annwn, where possible.

Give yourself 20 minutes uninterrupted time for this exercise. Create a safe and comfortable sacred space, in which ever way you prefer, and light a central candle for in honour of Cerridwen, as described earlier.

Take three deep breaths for water, three for air and three for land, and close your eyes or let your vision rest gently upon the candle flame, asserting your intention this time, to meet Creirwy.

Let your awareness soften and the room around you fade away and see yourself walking slowly towards the lake... it is a warm summers day and alongside the water is a broad field of long grasses and meadow flowers. The air hums with the buzzing of bees and you see a girl is sitting in the grass, weaving flowers together in her small nimble hands. As you approach, she looks up at you and smiles and you see her eyes are far wiser than she first appears. She stands and walks towards you, her features shifting and changing with each step, until she stands before you. Greet Creirwy respectfully, and offer her a flower. Spend some time in discussion with this sacred being, pay attention to how you feel in your body as you do so. What is it like to be so near to her? Let your conversation unfold as it will, paying attention to building relationship and seek to learn as much as you can about her, as well as yourself, at this time.

After a while the meeting will naturally come to a conclusion. Give her your thanks, and return the way you came. Letting your breath carry you, let the vision fade, and your spirit return to the room in which your body sits. Wiggle your toes and shake out your arms and hands to feel yourself back into your body. Close your sacred space and extinguish your candle, thanking Cerridwen for her tuition. Take some time to eat and drink to fully ground yourself back in the present, and record your experiences in your journal if you wish.

Morda

Morda, the old man whose task it is to stir the cauldron is another figure with a far greater importance than he would first appear. We are told in both Ellis Gruffydd's and Jones's versions that he is old and blind, but while Gruffydd doesn't name him, Jones reveals his name is in fact Morda. Morda is a variant of Mordaf, from the Celtic Marotamos.[21] Morda / Mordaf combines "mawr" (large, great) and the intensifying suffix -taf or -daf, so it means "the very great one". This seems to suggest this is a synonym for a god or other great figure, known to the audiences of these tales, who has yet to be identified. The figure of the blind old man is recurrent in world mythology, and such figures are usually considered to be seers or sages, the sense being that an inner vision has been gained by the loss of sight, in unison with the wisdom of great age and experience. Both Phineus from the tale of Jason and the Argonauts, and Tiresias, the blind prophet of Apollo can be found in Classical Greek Mythology, while in Norse myth the mysterious Odin offered up one of his eyes in order the learn the runes. His son, Höðr was blind and was tricked into slaying the hero Baldr.

When Cerridwen discovers that Gwion has received the three precious drops of potion and fled, she was said to be possessed by a frenzy, and hit Morda, knocking out one of his eyes. This makes him one eyed as well as blind, and is reminiscent of Odin once again. The image of the one-eyed man or supernatural being is seen multiple times in Norse as well as Celtic myth, where the Irish figure of Boann also loses one eye one arm and one leg in the pursuit of wisdom. Together with references to druids standing on one leg with one eye shut in order to prophesy, it seems to suggest somehow that the other eye (and leg) see (and stand) in the Otherworld or spirit realm, and that the figure dwells somehow between the two. So here we find that Morda is a powerful figure, perhaps one so well-known as to not be openly named, who walks between the worlds, and creates change by stirring and 'refining' as Gruffydd describes it, the great cauldron of life and death. In this Morda, like Odin, could be seen as a psychopomp figure, negotiating and 'refining' the process from life to death, sorting what remains and what is cast aside, and hinting perhaps at a mutual Indo-European source. In this sense Morda, of course, bears an even closer similarity to the Irish god the Dagda, who also is associated with a cauldron, and whose name bears a similarity in meaning "the good god" or "the great god", and is known among his other names as *Ruad Rofhessa* "mighty one/ lord of great knowledge". The Dagda in turn is also associated with Odin, and with the Irish ancestral god of the dead, Donn, as well as the Gaulish Sucellus. Sucellus is also attested in York, England as well as France, illustrating how wide-spread a figure he was during the Romano-Celtic period. In the figure of Morda we find all these figures hinted at, referred to subtly perhaps, without naming overtly, perhaps as just a memory of older now half-forgotten tradition, perhaps as an initiatory secret to be kept only by those seeking the cauldrons precious drops themselves. Morda as the blind fire tender and cauldron stirrer stokes the inner fire, the life force, so that is rises high enough to induce the vision or Awen, making the seeker Taliesin or 'radiant browed'.

Exercise: Meeting Morda
In this exercise we will be spending some time meditating on and perhaps meeting with Morda. Just as before, how deep this experience will be will depend very much on the individual. See this as a first step and an opportunity to meditate on the tale and those involved, and seek contact on the inner realms of Annwn, where possible.

Give yourself 20 minutes uninterrupted time for this exercise. Create a safe and comfortable sacred space, in which ever way you prefer, and light a central candle in honour of Cerridwen, as described earlier.

Take three deep breaths for water, three for air and three for land, and close your eyes or let your vision rest gently upon the candle flame, asserting your intention this time, to meet Morda.

Let your awareness soften and the room around you fade away and see yourself walking slowly towards the lake. By its edge, you see the fire and the cauldron above it, and standing beside the fire you see an old man. He wears a great cloak or shawl around his shoulders and he stares deep into your face – you see that one eye is white and blind, the other is a bright and dark – you sense he can see far more of you than what is merely on the surface of your appearance. The closer you come to him the more you sense this man is strange and unlike any other – he seems only partially here, the other side of his body shimmers as if it were seen through a heat haze. Yet there is still a sense of strength and great physicality about the man.

"I have travelled far to meet you here" he says. And motions for you to come and sit beside him.

Great the great one, with respect, and sit beside him for a while. Ask him about himself and how you may learn and find insight at this time. You may like to ask him as well about the fire and the cauldron, or about Cerridwen and Taliesin.

Let your conversation unfold as it will, paying attention to building relationship and seek to learn as much as you can about him, as well as yourself, at this time.

After a while the meeting will naturally come to a conclusion. Give him your thanks, and return the way you came. Letting your breath carry you, let the vision fade, and your spirit return to the room in which your body sits. Wiggle your toes and shake out your arms and hands to feel yourself back into your body. Close your sacred space and extinguish your candle, thanking Cerridwen for her tuition. Take some time to eat and drink to fully ground yourself back in the present, and record your experiences in your journal if you wish.

Gwion Bach

Gwion Bach, who becomes Taliesin after consuming the three drops of Cerridwen's brew, is also a highly significant figure in his own right. He is named as *Gwion Bach ap Gwreang* in John Jones' version of the tale, which means *'little bright or blessed seeing one, son of noble youth.'*[22] *Gwion* in Welsh is a variant of the name *Gwyn*, meaning *white or shining*, indicating something or someone holy, which comes from the Iron age Gaulish *vindos*, which in turn came from the Proto-Indo-European (PIE) root *weid* – meaning *"to see,"*[23] indicating magical or spiritual vision and knowledge, and wisdom. Bach in turn means small or not fully grown in Welsh, and ap means son of. Finally, *Gwreang* means young man or youth, but also indicates some nobility, such as a page or cupbearer at court. The implications of Taliesin to be, having the name of 'little blessed holy seer, son of noble youth' suggests that his imbibing of the magical brew of inspiration was intended all along, that he occupies an already significant position as the pre-initiated, the chosen child. His accompaniment by the ancient Morda, the 'very great one' implies now some form of teacher and student pattern, seeking and tending to the fires of inner vision together, paying their dues to the initiatrix herself who stands apart at this stage and yet is the ultimate authority. More on this later.

Gwion and his form as the reborn baby Taliesin, is an excellent example of a recurring motif in the Celtic tradition, that of the wondrous child, who is born with the wisdom of the ancients, the memory of all things…a consciously reincarnated soul if you will. The figures of Gwion / Taliesin and Cerridwen finds similarities in other Welsh tales especially, most notably Pryderi the son of Rhiannon and Mabon son of Modron (meaning son of the mother) who finds their sources in the earlier Iron age Celtic cults of the divine mothers, known as the *Matres*, and in the figures of Maponus and Matrona respectively. The theme of the son having to leave the mother as a baby plays out in the story of Pryderi and Rhiannon as an abduction, but there is a pattern here none the less that speaks of a far earlier mystery teaching or tale which finds is echoes scattered across the oral tradition.

Gwion's name, 'bright / blessed one' is cognate with the Irish Fionn,[24] and their tales have striking similarities. Fionn mac Cumhail, rather than a bard, was a warrior magician, leader of a group of heroes called the Fianna. He gained his magical skills as a boy when he was set to work for an old man, who was cooking the Salmon of Knowledge over a fire, in order to consume it and receive its Imbas, or magical inspiration, the Irish version of the Awen. At the last minute, the cooking salmon has a bubble arise on its skin, which Ffion pushes down with his thumb, burning himself. He then sucks his thumb and the magical Imbas is given to him instead of his master. Ffion's tale written down in the 9th Century, probably predates that of Gwion in its first written form, but it is likely they both draw their sources from earlier oral traditions now lost. The concept of a bright or blessed one, the golden child of wonder, who carries with him wisdom from the other world or functions as a reincarnated ascended spirit, certainly goes back to the very earliest times.

Exercise: Meeting Gwion / Taliesin

In this exercise we will be spending some time meditating on and perhaps meeting Gwion / Taliesin as an initiate of Cerridwen's traditional cult. Just as before, how deep this experience will be will depend very much on the individual. See this as a first step and an opportunity to meditate on the tale and those involved, and seek contact on the inner realms of Annwn, where possible.

Give yourself 20 minutes uninterrupted time for this exercise. Create a safe and comfortable sacred space, in which ever way you prefer, and light a central candle in honour of Cerridwen, as described earlier.

Take three deep breaths for water, three for air and three for land, and close your eyes or let your vision rest gently upon the candle flame, asserting your intention this time, to meet Gwion / Taliesin.

See yourself standing by the lakeside, surrounded by the blue light or either dusk or dawn – what time of day do you feel it to be? For this is the day when Gwion becomes Taliesin. Walk along the lakeside until you see the cauldron hanging over the fire, and a figure with bright golden hair glowing by its side. Greet the bard as teacher and wise one. He will have much to impart if you create the space for him to do so. How does he appear to you at this time?

Walk along the edge of the lake and allow Gwion / Taliesin, however he comes to you, to impart the wisdom he chooses at this time. Which side of his transformation he comes to you in, will dictate much of what transpires and perhaps will say much in and of itself. Remember to ask him how he sees time and how he draws his wisdom from the Otherworld – see if he will advise you in connecting further with Cerridwen. How does he see his muse and mistress at this time? What words will he offer you to help develop your own Awen at this time?

Let your conversation unfold as it will, paying attention to building relationship and seek to learn as much as you can about him, as well as yourself, at this time.

After a while the meeting will naturally come to a conclusion. Give him your thanks, and return the way you came. Letting your breath carry you, let the vision fade, and your spirit return to the room in which your body sits. Wiggle your toes and shake out your arms and hands to feel yourself back into your body. Close your sacred space and extinguish your candle, thanking Cerridwen for her tuition. Take some time to eat and drink to fully ground yourself back in the present, and record your experiences in your journal if you wish.

Gwion/Taliesin fire in the head

Landscape and Local Gods

Now we have discussed the main characters in the tale, let us now turn our attention to the landscape and the physical aspects of the story. When we consider each of these elements, we may find they hold significant features which hold clues as to their parts in the initiation of Taliesin, and by extension, for us as well in our search for connection with Cerridwen.

The Mountains and the Lake

Throughout the Celtic nations and around the world there is a tradition of going to high places and mountain tops to seek the wisdom of the spirits or the gods. High places seem to hold an energy of their own, separate from the world of humans where a greater vision can be found. Many mountains in Britain and Ireland are associated with giants, which it is thought, were once considered gods. Cadair Idris, the chair of the giant Idris in Snowdonia is one such place, where tradition holds that should you sleep upon its summit you will be rendered dead, mad, or a poet by morning. The summit of Cadair Idris is thought to look somewhat like a great throne, a place for the giant to sit, but it is notable that the term 'chair' is also used in the bardic traditions to represent a position of authority, from which the bard recounts their wisdom. Near the summit of Cadair Idris is a lake *Llyn Cau,* which sits like a bowl or cauldron, reflecting the sky.

Cerridwen's husband is Tegid Foel, Tegid/ Fair bald one, signifying the perhaps the mountain tops that can be seen on the westerly horizon, from the shores of Llyn Tegid, Bala Lake. The water from Llyn Tegid finds its source high in the mountains, from the river Dee which springs from Dduallt mountain, in the heart of the mountain range. According to folklore[25] his court was said to be beneath the waters of Llyn Tegid, after having been drowned in a single day. Another tale, as discussed earlier, was that there was a holy well at the centre of his court, which was hidden in a sacred enclosure, but one day the guardian of the well failed in their duty and the devil visited, overflowing the land with its waters. We see here the same motif of the cauldron and its breaking after Gwion consumed the drops of inspiration, as well as a sense perhaps that the earlier pre-Christian traditions practiced are enclosed and hidden away from prying eyes, accessible only by traversing the waters and seeking entry into the Otherworld. There is a long tradition, especially in Wales, of accessing the realm of the spirits or finding the Otherworld Annwn, beneath the waters of a lake, and many Otherworldly figures in folktales come from beneath a lake in order to support or sometimes endanger those in the local area. The name of the Otherworld in Welsh, Annwn, means 'the deep place' alluding to this, as well as perhaps a sense of depth psychologically and emotionally/ spiritually – accessible therefore via a change in consciousness.

So, in the presence of the mountains, we have a seat or chair of the gods, and to the east we have a sacred lake, and from which secret initiations may occur, away from the everyday world. The waters from these mountain peaks descend to form the great cauldron that is Llyn Tegid, the fair lake, where Cerridwen, the wife of the mountain god, brews her potion of inspiration.

Llyn Tegid, the fair lake, can be seen as a vast cauldron in its own right. Perhaps this was in fact Cerridwen's cauldron itself – a site of initiatory process. Many lakes were places of offering and ritual in the bronze and Iron Age, where the waters of the Otherworld provide reflection of the realms above. The largest body of water in Wales, Llyn Tegid holds a great deal of aquatic life, including its own species of white fish, the *gwyniad*, which are fished for food. The lake and its source bring water to the fields and homes of all the people in the area, making it a cauldron of plenty indeed. In the folklore, on moonlit nights and to certain seekers, the lake allow access to Tegids court, to the Otherworld Annwn, from which great wisdom can be brought back for the service of the community and the inner vision of its initiates.

The River

The river Dee, Afon Dyfrdwy, which finds it source high in the mountains, descends the foothills to feed Llyn Tegid. The river itself is an often-overlooked aspect of this tale, despite its highly significant name. There are five river Dee's in Britain and Ireland – one in Cumbria England, two in Scotland, one in the republic of Ireland and one in Wales. The repetition of this name, Dee, is significant, and while the source of its use in every instance is unclear, (especially with the Irish river Dee which takes its name from the hero Ferdiad, which may or may not be related), we do have some intriguing clues to suggest is great antiquity and importance. In Scotland, we find a reference to the river Dee, which flows to the sea at Aberdeen (also named after it) at a very early date in the second century writings of Ptolemy, in his *Roman Britain* where he refers to the river as Δηουανα Devona. Devona is taken to either mean goddess, or perhaps relates to the possible Gallo-Roman goddess Divona (Gaulish: Deuona, Diuona, 'Divine', from *deuos*, meaning god). In addition, Giraldus Cambrensis spells the name of the Welsh river Dee, as *Deverdoeu*, where doeu is the same as the old Welsh doiu or duiu, the genitive of old Welsh *diu*, a god. It is unclear whether Divona was a title for a series of river and freshwater goddesses, or one goddess honoured over a broad area, as there are several references to their worship in Europe. The fourth century Roman poet Ausonius also refers to Divona as being a Celtic name for a river goddess in Europe. I think we can assume that all the river Dee's in Britain are named from Devona as a title for their own local river goddess, whose name may have been a hidden cult secret. We can then see that its highly significant that the Welsh river Dee flows into Llyn Tegid. Given the animistic beliefs of Celts and early Britons, we may see that originally the river itself, was considered a goddess, sacred and divine, its holy waters forming the cauldron of the Otherworld, and perhaps revealing to us how very ancient this myth and initiatory tale may be in its earliest incarnations.

To the Iron Age Celts of Europe as well as in Britain and Ireland, rivers and springs held a special significance as the embodiments of their own local river deities. These were usually feminine, and were seen as both beneficent and terrible, overseeing entrance to the Otherworld, they could be called upon for healing, divination and even for cursing, and received regular offerings and most likely ceremony. A great many of these sites have been studied by archaeologists and the offerings uncovered are rich and varied, from swords and other rich metal artifacts, to coins and even models of eyes and other body parts in need of healing. At the healing springs at Bath, Somerset UK, rolled curse tablets made of lead were also found. We therefore can consider that Devona, or Dee the river goddess was equally a mix of darkness and light, life and death, and beneath it, and initiation into the underworld or Annwn, much as we may understand Cerridwen today.

Devona and Aerwen

What more can we know about this mysterious goddess of the river Dee? One of the versions of the birth of Taliesin, is as discussed earlier, is the *Hanes Taliesin* recorded by John Jones of Gellilyfdy (circa 1607) which contains several details not included in the more for famous Elis Gruffydd version. In his version, Jones says *"ai ymchwelud tu ag afon Ayrwem* (and chased him towards the river Aerwen)." Here we find the hidden goddess name of the river. The name Aerwen is still found in the area above Bala, and is also considered in local lore as an old name for the river Dee. Aerwen is also spelled as Aerfen, and both versions are drawn from the proto-Celtic word *agrona* 'Slaughter" making "slaughter goddess'[26] or 'woman of slaughter". When one thinks of a battle goddess connected to a river or lake, its connection with the traditions of making offerings of swords and other weapons and warrior accoutrements to bodies of water in the Bronze and Iron Age is quite a natural next step, as is the connection with the story of the giantess who first had the Welsh Cauldron of Rebirth, the *Pair Dadeni*, which is mentioned in the tale of Brân and Branwen in the second branch of the *Mabinogi*. The giantess Cymidei Cymeinfoll, 'pregnant in war/ pregnant with war' came, it was said, from a lake in Ireland called 'the lake of the cauldron.' She was said to give birth to a fully formed warrior every six weeks, and she and her husband would throw dead warriors into their cauldron, from which they would arise living but mute – unable to say what they had seen in the realm of the dead. The war goddess on the Gundestrup cauldron, throwing warriors into a great cauldron from which warriors also emerge, also springs to mind here. The similarities between all three are unmistakable, and the connection perhaps to Cerridwen's cauldron are tantalising indeed. Yet again we see glimpses of a far earlier tradition – we have pieces of a lost mystery tradition which can tempt us into seeing a vision of a whole which, without further archaeological evidence, we will always be unable to definitively prove. Was Gwion's initiation at the hands of Cerridwen, to seek the Awen, a late version of a warrior initiation? Could the 'enlightenment' the magical and spiritual knowledge that the Awen offers, in this Medieval version of the tale, be something sought in the earlier warrior culture of the Iron Age and perhaps even earlier? Certainly, many martial arts that we know in the world today have a thread of spirituality or mysticism flowing through their history and sometimes this is still overt in their modern practice, such as the relationship between Buddhism and Kung-fu. For now, we can sense a pattern, but we can never know for sure with our rational minds.

Exercise: Journey to Meet Aerwen

In this exercise we will be spending some time meditating on and perhaps meeting with Aerwen. Just as before, how deep this experience will be will depend very much on the individual. See this as a first step and an opportunity to meditate on the tale and those involved, and seek contact on the inner realms of Annwn, where possible.

Give yourself 20 minutes uninterrupted time for this exercise. Create a safe and comfortable sacred space, in which ever way you prefer, and light a central candle in honour of Cerridwen, as described earlier.

Take three deep breaths for water, three for air and three for land, and close your eyes or let your vision rest gently upon the candle flame, asserting your intention this time, to meet Aerwen.

Let your awareness soften and the room around you fade away and see yourself walking slowly towards the river, surrounded by the high mountains of Eryri (Snowdonia) it makes it way sometimes loud as it tumbles over rocks, sometimes slower and deeper... at the rivers edge bow your head a moment and greet the river goddess, Aerwen. She may come to you in any form, and invite you to join her in the cold fast running waters, falling into the deep dark depths... this ancient one is as young as a moment and as old as the mountains, but most of all she is proud and fierce, she takes people from their ordinary lives and makes them a warrior, one who knows death and what lies beyond.

At some point you descend into a place of still darkness, and you feel mortal life falling away, meaningless. Sadness comes and goes as she washes away the life you had known. Let the dark stillness in for a while, let this falling away become something you can trust like the leaves falling from the trees. As you vision fills with more and more darkness and stillness you suddenly see a light, glinting far below you. Do you choose to go further? Far below is Aerwen again, her eyes the only thing that seem illuminated in this place of endings.

She speaks, with a voice of swords clashing and waterfalls thundering over rocks "what will you give me, here in this place?"

You reach out and give her something – it comes to you unbidden, something to feel rather than overly think on. It is something that is intrinsically you and yours, without words or a name. it is like your will, or your spirit, or your courage, yet it is all of these things and none of them, something deeper. She takes it from you with hands as cold as snowmelt.

In her hands your gift, shapeless and unformed, begins to glow as if it burns in her presence, she moves her hands over it, reshaping, reforming it, and it begins to glow brighter and brighter, with a red gold flame. Finally, she passes it through the darkness, and it hisses like something new forged cooled in cold water, shining now cooler, silver or bronze light glimmering in the darkness. She holds it out and tells you to look at it closely...what do you see reflected there? You must never tell another what you see, or the words she speaks now. This is the sacred rule of the cauldron.

Finally, she hands your gift back to you, changed for ever by her skilful hands.

"Go" she says, with a voice like the ringing of metal on an anvil and the hiss of rain water on hot stone.

You bow to her and rise up through the waters until you see sunlight and you climb up, easily with new vigour in your muscles, up out of the water and onto the river bank. Changed, and yet the same.

Letting your breath carry you, let the vision fade, and your spirit return to the room in which your body sits. Wiggle your toes and shake out your arms and hands to feel yourself back into your body. Close your sacred space and extinguish your candle, thanking Cerridwen for her tuition. Take some time to eat and drink to fully ground yourself back in the present, and record your experiences in your journal if you wish.

The Fire

Another key aspect of the tale of Cerridwen is the fire that must be kept lit beneath the cauldron, tended for a year by Gwion and

Morda. So, the fair chosen child, and the great one, master and student, tend the fire of Cerridwen's cauldron, seeing that it is fed and kept alight without faltering. A fire must be prepared for in a specific way, laid with care, with tinder and kindling, before bringing a spark and encouraging it into a flame. In the same way, knowledge and teaching tales may serve as the tinder and kindling, to take the divine spark of inspiration and spirit presence, so that it can grow into inner illumination of the mysteries, growing into a fire through the application of time and practice, lived experience. Spiritual paths around the world talk of building up the inner fire, such as the kundalini traditions of India, and here we see the teacher and the student building the fire up and tending to it with consistency, patience and care, in the service of Cerridwen, for the span and turn of a whole year before the initiation is achieved and fully undergone.

Fire has a special place in the Celtic traditions. The four main festivals of the Celts, held on the cross-quarter days in between the solstices and equinoxes, known in Welsh as *Gŵyl Forwyn*, or *Gŵyl Fair y Canhwyllau*, (1st or 2nd of Feb) *Calan Mai* (1st of May), *Gŵyl Awst* (1st Aug), and *Calan Gaeaf* (31st Oct) are all associated with fire, and fire was used as a blessing and cleansing force in many rituals, where it was seen as reflecting what we would call today the life force of the earth. The name Taliesin meaning 'radiant brow' can be seen to indicate that his life force or inner fire had risen to such an extent that he was divinely gifted, speaking with the life force or soul of the land itself.

The Animal Transformations

In this section we will look at each of Taliesin and Cerridwen's animal transformations, and consider their context in wider Celtic traditions as well as explore them for insights into our own spiritual practice.

Hare (Welsh: Ysgyfarnog)

In his escape from Cerridwen, Taliesin shapeshifts, *'yn rhith ysgyfarnog'*, (in the form of a hare). The only type of hare known in Wales is the brown hare, *Lepus europaeus* that was introduced into Britain by the Romans. At first glance hares may appear to look similar to rabbits but the differences are clear when you take a little time. Hares are far larger than rabbits, up to 48–70cm in length and 3–5kg in weight. While rabbits live in groups underground in burrows, hares live above ground, preferring open fields. The hair on a hare is a warmer brown than you will see on a rabbit which usually has greyish brown fur, and hares have black-tipped ears which are twice the length of their head, whereas a rabbit's brown ears are relatively short. Hares also have longer legs than rabbits and seem to leap more than a rabbit's 'hop' as they run through the fields – where they can reach an astonishing 45 miles per hour, often running in a zig zag pattern to evade a predator. Especially in March, the mating season, hares can sometimes be seen 'boxing' rearing up and hitting each other's paws and heads. This is to assert dominance among males as well as female hares, known as jills, fighting off unwanted suitors. Sometimes several males will chase and box a female to win the right to mate with her.

Hares have a long history of magical associations, being connected with the moon in Asian, Classical and indigenous American folklore. In northern Europe especially in Celtic areas like Wales Scotland and Ireland, hares are associated with witches and shapeshifting. Many a tale has been told about old women turning into hares on moonlit nights, often to steal the luck or fertility off a neighbouring farm – in Ireland these were called butter witches and stole the virtue of goodness off the milk as well as stealing the fertility and prosperity of the farm itself. In Scotland, the witch trials record the wisewoman Isobel Gowdie testifying that she turned into a hare, with the help of the devil, after her pact with the king and queen of the fairies. Her shapeshifting charm is recorded thus;

I shall go into a hare,
With sorrow and sych and meickle care;
And I shall go in the Devil's name,
Ay while I come home again.

To change back, she would say:

Hare, hare, God send thee care.
I am in a hare's likeness now,
But I shall be in a woman's likeness even now.[27]

To begin the shapeshifting section of the tale by Gwion turning into a hare places the story firmly in this tradition and would have announced to those hearing the tale in person that this is a story about magical initiations and traditions, in effect it illustrates that Gwion is mid-way through training as a native magical practitioner.

In Wales there is a female saint closely associated with the hare. Saint Melangell is the Welsh patron saint of hares, and she was said to have lived as a hermitess, a wild woman alone in the forest after fleeing Ireland where her father was trying to force her to marry. Her saint's day is May 27th. One day the Prince of Powys whose name was Brochwel Yscythrog, was out hunting with his hounds, when they chased a hare into a thicket. They pursued it, but found the hare sitting at the feet of a woman, Melangell, in the folds of her dress. The prince tried to urge the hounds to attack the hare but they wouldn't, and then he spoke to Melangell, awed by her devotion to God. The prince let the hare go, and declared that Melangell could have all the land around her as a sanctuary for any who came there. Interestingly, this seems to have echoes with the story of the Iceni queen Boudicca, five centuries older, who instead of having a hare sit in her skirts, released a hare from the folds of her cloak as a form of divination, perhaps in offering to the goddess of victory Andraste before she led her people on a revolt against the Roman occupation of Britain.

It's worth mentioning here that the hare as well as being a magical creature, is also a creature of earth, and the lands fertility, mating, as it does, as the first crops begin turn the bare fields green. Hares are also clever fast animals, known to evade capture and go unseen seemingly in plain sight – again, these are markers of spiritual / magical initiation, the knowing of secrets and hidden knowledge whilst seemingly living in the ordinary world. A good spirit animal to invoke should you wish to avoid capture, but also one who is privy to secrets and is keen in the pursuit of its goals. If Melangell's hare has any relevance in the tale of Gwion / Taliesin it is about evading pursuit and finding secret ways, but also perhaps about invoking a sanctuary, or delineating the boundaries of a sacred ritual or pursuit, setting it apart from the rigours of the everyday world and placing it firmly in the realms of the spiritual and magical. The tale of Melangell, whose feast day was recorded in the year 590 CE, around the time the historical Taliesin could have been alive, is probably drawn from earlier and even pre-Christian sources. Her tale has echoes of the importance and sanctity of the wild and of the earlier goddess and genius loci (local divinities) who were said to preside over specific rivers and mountains throughout the Celtic world. Like Cerridwen, we have the story here of a woman who held power over a specific area and was the guardian of a spiritual tradition – be it the magical initiations of the *Awen*, or the spiritual sanctuary provided by the (now Christian) God. Perhaps here we find two pieces of the same picture, now lost to time, with the connecting parts long gone but enough remaining to give us a tantalising guess at a wider spread native belief.

Exercise: Running with the Hare

Give yourself 20 minutes uninterrupted time for this exercise. Create a safe and comfortable sacred space, in which ever way you prefer, and light a central candle for in honour of Cerridwen, as described earlier.

Take three deep breaths for water, three for air and three for land, and close your eyes or let your vision rest gently upon the candle flame.

Let your outer awareness fade, and using your inner vision see yourself seated on the rich grass beside the lake, with a vast moon in a deep blue sky above you. Let yourself sink in to the atmosphere, feel the earth beneath you, its deep and wild fertility, the secret things that run and hunt on the rich land now the night has come. Feel the night air stir around you, the shelter of the long grasses around you, shushing gently in a soft breeze. Let the scene form strongly around you, and then in your own words, ask the land to send the spirit of the hare to you, in friendship, that you may learn its wisdom.

Across the grass, coming like a swift shadow, the hare approaches, fixing you with its wide black eye. You stare at each other for a while, the air seeming to fill with unspoken words between you, and you begin to feel your body shift and change. You feel your feet become paws, and your ears lengthen, taking in all the sounds and ripples or air that are carried for miles around you. Your human form slips away and you feel light and swift, one with the wildness of the earth. The hare turns, looking at you once with its bright stare, and runs off ahead of you into the night, pulling you with it along its wild and secret ways.

Let the hare guide you. Let yourself run and leap and be one with it. Trust its strangeness, let yourself feel the currents of the moon which guide it, stirring its blood, reflected in the blackness of its eyes. Let yourself know what it is to be prey, and yet one with all around you, fierce hearted. Fleet of foot.

Remember that every act in the Otherworld, every moment in communion with another being is its own tuition and blessing, so let this time unfold as it will. It is its own treasure.

After a while you will be led back to the rich grass beside the lake.
Give your thanks to the hare spirit and gently see your hands and feet
returning to their human form, your body and spirit back and whole
as it was before and is every day.

Thank the land beneath you, and using your breath, let the vision
fade, and your spirit return to the room in which your body sits.
Wiggle your toes and shake out your arms and hands to feel yourself
back into your body. Close your sacred space and extinguish your
candle, thanking Cerridwen for her tuition. Take some time to eat and
drink to fully ground yourself back in the present, and record your
experiences in your journal if you wish.

The Greyhound (Welsh: Miliast)

In response to Taliesin fleeing as a hare, Cerridwen pursues him
"in rhith miliast ddu," (into the form of a black greyhound bitch).
The hound in the tale is usually described as a greyhound, but
this wouldn't be a greyhound as we know them today. Rather,
this is a generic term used in medieval literature to describe
a variety of hunting dog breeds, most of which would have
been far larger and fiercer, more like an Irish wolfhound, than a
modern greyhound is today. A 'greyhound' or a pack of hounds,
was the classic medieval courtly accessory for the princes and
aristocracy of the era, to use when hunting but also as a status
symbol. These courtly hunts weren't for food although they may
provide it, rather they were for sport and could be seen as a way
to demonstrate power over the landscape, given that hunting
rights were denied to the lower status members of society. Such
hounds were often highly regarded as trusty companions to
their owners and were sometimes treated, and certainly fed,
better than the servants.

Hounds feature strongly in Celtic myth and folklore, often as
accompaniments to the Otherworldly Wild Hunt, a procession
of spirits including fairies and the dead which would scour
the land on stormy winter nights. The Wild Hunt was led by

the Wild Huntsman, a figure that recurs throughout European myth but in Wales is usually seen as either Arawn, as recorded in the collection of stories known as the *Mabinogi*, or Gwyn ap Nudd, who is known as a king of fairy and the lord of the Welsh Otherworld, Annwfn (Annwn is its modern spelling). Gwyn in folklore is accompanied by his hound Dormach of the ruddy nose,[28] which is red from eating the blood and gore of the dead. Annwfn, as the Welsh Otherworld is also considered to be the land of the dead, and hounds have an association with the dead and the 'underworld' throughout European lore, as guardians and protectors.

Hounds feature frequently in Iron Age and earlier burial traditions, and some occasions have been buried in all honour, sometimes with signs that they were ritually sacrificed perhaps to protect the land in which they are buried. Dog burials next to humans, presumably their owners, have also been found several times, especially in the Neolithic era. This suggests they were intended to accompany their owners in their journey to the next world. Dogs also feature in hunting scenes on the Gundestrup Cauldron. In one scene of on the cauldron, as already discussed there is a line of warriors being held at bay by a large dog, behind which, there is a figure, possibly a woman, who is twice the size of the others, seemingly placing a warrior into a large cauldron, from which other warriors, on horseback, have emerged. This scene is reminiscent of the cauldron of rebirth, the *Pair Dadeni*, owned by Bendigeidfran, Bran the blessed, which was used by the Irish King Matholwch to regenerative his fallen warriors, in the second branch of the *Mabinogi*. This cauldron was once owned by a warrior giantess – perhaps a long-forgotten war goddess, Cymidei Cymeinfoll, as discussed later. Again, we see similarities with the scene depicted in the Gundestrup cauldron.

For Cerridwen to turn into a hound in the pursuit of Gwion-as-hare, we see her as the fierce protectress and hunter of the

Otherworld, Annwfn, the challenger whose pursuit of her prey provides initiation via the strength to overcome and endure her ferocity. In taking the form of the hound, she positions herself as the companion to the lord of the Wild Hunt and of the Welsh realm of the dead, entry to which can only be achieved by her permission. The resonances here between the Gundestrup cauldron and the cauldron of rebirth in the second branch of the *Mabinogi* are startling, suggesting that Cerridwen holds a similar role, negotiating the seekers initiation and rebirth within the cauldron itself.

Exercise: Running with the Hound

Give yourself 20 minutes uninterrupted time for this exercise. Create a safe and comfortable sacred space, in which ever way you prefer, and light a central candle in honour of Cerridwen, as described earlier.

Take three deep breaths for water, three for air and three for land, and close your eyes or let your vision rest gently upon the candle flame.

Let your outer awareness fade, and using your inner vision see yourself seated on the rich grass beside the lake, the sun is warm on your body and you feel how alive everything is around you, the earth and all the growing things, the sigh and ripples of the lake beside you, the rush and chatter of the river not far off. After a while, ask the rich earth beneath you, to bring to you a hound, to be your guide in friendship, that you may learn its wisdom.

Immediately, you see a shape bounding towards you across the turf, and a large wolfhound approaches, with a strong muscular body and rich brown shaggy hair. It comes to a halt beside you and stands proud, its head raised. You gaze slowly into its deep brown eyes, warm as a tilled field, and feel a shift come across you. Your body changes and grows, filling with strength and the vibrant aliveness of the hound before you. The hound opens its huge jaws revealing its large white teeth in a great yawn of greeting, and the two of you run off across the soft green grass beside the river.

Follow the hound for a while, trust in its wisdom, and the knowing in its body. Let yourself explore this rich sacred landscape as one fully embodied, able to follow the tracks between this world and the other. Let yourself be one with its pack, moving as one body through the landscape. Delight in your strength and agility, your easy ferocity. Let the hound teach you what it is to be one of them.

Remember that every act in the Otherworld, every moment in communion with another being is its own tuition and blessing, so let this time unfold as it will. It is its own treasure.

After a while you will be led back to the rich grass beside the lake. Give your thanks to the hound spirit and gently see your hands and feet returning to their human form, your body and spirit back and whole as it was before and is every day.

Thank the land beneath you, and using your breath, let the vision fade, and your spirit return to the room in which your body sits. Wiggle your toes and shake out your arms and hands to feel yourself back into your body. Close your sacred space and extinguish your candle, thanking Cerridwen for her tuition. Take some time to eat and drink to fully ground yourself back in the present, and record your experiences in your journal if you wish.

The Fish (Welsh: Pysgod, or salmon – eog)

After being chased as a hare, by Cerridwen-as-hound, Gwion/ Taliesin turns himself into a fish *"yn bysgodyn"* (into a fish) and dives into a river, usually taken to be the Afon Dyfrdwy, or its older name, Afon Ayrwem.[29] Fish are magical creatures in all Celtic mythology, able to travel to and from the realms of the Otherworld, often by the fact that they dwell in the water, which is seen, especially in Wales as offering access to Annwn,[30] 'the deep place'. The water element was always considered to be connected to spirits, fairies (Tylwyth teg) and the old gods, but while it was feared it was also seen as a place from where blessing could come to the mortal world. The fish in the tale of Taliesin, is usually considered to be the salmon, the most famous type of fish in Celtic and Welsh mythology which also finds special importance in Ireland. The salmon features in the tale of Culhwch and Olwen, where the salmon of Llyn Llyw is said to be the oldest creature in the world, and the only being to know where the hero / God Mabon ap Modron is imprisoned.[31] The salmon in the tale is a mighty being indeed, having pulled the eagle of Gwernabwy, who had travelled the most in all the world, under the waters of his lake when the eagle tried to hunt him. He was so large and strong that he was able to carry the heroes Kai and Gwrhyr Gwalstawd upon his shoulders, to where Mabon was held.[32]

The salmon also features strongly in the Irish tradition, as the salmon of knowledge, which ate the hazel nuts at the well of Segais, the well of wisdom, as already discussed. The Irish hero magician Fionn mac Cumhail, who also bears similarities to the figure of Taliesin, was said to have gained his magical wisdom and abilities from tasting the salmon, when he was attending its cooking, on behalf of the poet / magician Finn Eces (or Finegas) in a tale with many similarities with that of Gwion serving Cerridwen. The salmon also features in the Irish in the tale of Fintan mac Bóchra, or Fintan the wise, who was a seer or magician. In Irish pseudo-history / mythology, he accompanied the granddaughter of Noah, Cessair, to Ireland after the great flood, and lived in the form of a salmon for a year among his many adventures.

Here we see the interchange of ideas across the Irish sea, as well as perhaps hinting at earlier tradition, but the figure of Taliesin turning into a salmon as part of his transformations seems entirely fitting as an initiation to the newly wise and divinely inspired. Embodying the oldest of animals, perhaps even being accompanied by it as a spirit ally, Gwion swims into the very deep place itself, Annwfn, the womb of the world. Here the lines between the self and all of creation may seem to blur and merge, and the old Gwion may fall away and become something new, the inner radiance of Taliesin, may be discovered like a pearl in the depths.

Exercise: Swimming with the Salmon

Give yourself 20 minutes uninterrupted time for this exercise. Create a safe and comfortable sacred space, in which ever way you prefer, and light a central candle in honour of Cerridwen, as described earlier.

Take three deep breaths for water, three for air and three for land, and close your eyes or let your vision rest gently upon the candle flame.

Let your outer awareness fade, and using your inner vision see yourself seated at the edge of the river which winds its way down to Llyn Tegid, the lake, watching the water rushing by below you. in your inner ear, you may be able to hear the rush and rhythm of the water as it tumbles and eddies along making its way endlessly to the sea. Let your attention sink into the water and loosen your connection to the here and now.

After a while, ask the river, in your own words, to bring to you a salmon guide, that you may swim together and learn the wisdom of the salmon. Gently, let your feet dangle over the river, and let your toes rest upon the water, before you sink slowly inch by inch into its depths. The water is cool, and the light from above filters through lighting everything a gentle, pale living green, like early spring. As you feel the water slip over your head, you are aware that you can breathe perfectly well, and that a great shimmering form has approached you. This is your salmon guide, sent from the great salmon of Llyn Llyw, the oldest being in the world. It circles you and you feel its shimmery, silvery smooth sides brush against you, and you realise that you too are a salmon, for just a while. Your guide leads you off along the brisk and bubbling currents of the river, swim and flow with them allowing the current of events to unfold its wisdom for you.

Remember that every act in the Otherworld, every moment in communion with another being is its own tuition and blessing, so let this time unfold as it will. It is its own treasure.

After a while you will be led back to the river bank. Give your thanks to the salmon spirit and gently see your hands and feet returning to their human form, your body and spirit back and whole as it was before and is every day.

Thank the river, and using your breath, let the vision fade, and your spirit return to the room in which your body sits. Wiggle your toes and shake out your arms and hands to feel yourself back into your body. Close your sacred space and extinguish your candle, thanking Cerridwen for her tuition. Take some time to eat and drink to fully ground yourself back in the present, and record your experiences in your journal if you wish.

The Otter (Welsh: Dwrgi, dyfrast – she otter)

Watching otters in the wild is a pleasure, as they move in such fluid ways from land to water, they are both playful and affectionate to each other. However, to their prey they are highly effective predators, giving them their reputation as being 'water dogs'. Mostly nocturnal, the animals are very shy and hard to find, though their presence in an area can be identified due to their prints, and their spraint as well as the shells of the mussels and other crustaceans that provide much of their diet. While sea otters feed on salt water shellfish mostly, fresh water otters which live in the rivers and lakes of Wales and throughout the UK will eat mostly fish such as trout and salmon, as well as eels. They will also hunt on land, eating birds, bird's eggs, insects and small mammals. In many ways, the otter is an 'in-between' liminal creature, best seen at the in-between times of dawn and dusk, and traveling in-between the realms of land and water – this world and the Otherworld.

As already seen, when Gwion / Taliesin takes on the form of a fish, Cerridwen pursues him *yn rrith dyfrast* 'into the form of a she-otter'. Having first changed into the form of land-dwelling animals they have now shifted to the realm of water, with Gwion as the salmon, associated with wisdom, Cerridwen's form, however, is one that can travel on and or in water, and like the hound, is a formidable predator to its prey. Otters have a strong presence in Celtic and Welsh folklore, though lesser known than the salmon and the hound. In Scotland the otter is known as the 'dratsie' and there are said to be silver 'otter kings' that are accompanied by seven black otters. When captured the otter king would grant a wish in return for his freedom. Their skins were said to be impenetrable and were highly sought after by warriors as it was said to make someone invincible. Otter kings were also known in Irish lore where they are also known as the Dobhar-chú, (water dog). In Wales the otter is closely associated with the beaver, and the mythical monster, the Afanc. (The English words 'water' and 'otter' are both derived from the Greek hydr 'water', hydros 'small water animal', and hydra 'water-serpent'. In this way we can see how the Welsh and English words for these creatures join up in their earlier Indo-European roots.)

Afanc is the Welsh word for beaver, which were found in the British Isles until the 13th Century (they are now being re-introduced) but in Welsh oral lore and literature the word has always been used as a term for a water monster. The word afanc is derived from the proto-Celtic word for river, which in modern Welsh is *afon* (Breton – *avon*, Irish *abhainn*). However, while the word for river and for beaver / otter are related, as an afanc, it is distinctly some kind of supernatural river spirit or monster, of which there are numerous examples throughout the all the Celtic traditions. Indeed, in folklore an Afanc or water monster is also said to dwell in Llyn Tegid/ Bala Lake, revealing another surviving thread of the story. According to the renowned Celtic scholar John Koch the earliest attestation for the word afanc as a monster is from the 9th century, under the Latinized Old Breton form *abacus*.[33] The word Afanc is often combined with the word for black – dhu, giving us afagddu or y fagddu 'utter darkness' in Modern Welsh, and, of course, one of the names of Cerridwen's son/s. (As already discussed, in *Ystoria Taliesin* (Gruffydd) Cerridwen's son is named Afagddu due to his ugliness, whereas in the John Jones version, the *Hanes Taliesin*, Afagddu is the nickname of Morfran.) An alternative spelling, *Addanc* is found in the tale of the Arthurian knight Peredur, where he comes across a man who has been slain by an addanc, riding on a horse. The women take the slain man and bathe his body in a tub of water in a motif reminiscent of the cauldron of regeneration, from which the man arises alive once more. Peredur then goes on to slay the addanc. The afanc also appears in numerous other Welsh folktales, and place names, such as Bedd yr Afanc (the afanc's grave) near Brynberian, Pembrokeshire, and Llyn yr Afanc, a pool on the river Conwy. In this way we can see that the idea of Cerridwen turning into a she-otter, is intimately linked with ideas of the other world, river and water spirits and monsters, and is perhaps a continuation of some thread found in the name of her son.

The significance of the otter goes back a long way to the Romano-Celtic period if not earlier. The Gaulish water goddess Damona is also connected to otters, as in the archaeological remains of her veneration in Alesia, (Burgundy France) she if often partnered with the Gallo-Roman deity Apollo Moritasgus. Mori-tazgos is a Celtic animal name, literally signifying 'sea-badger', the sea otter. Otters are also a feature in the Irish Voyage of St Brendan, where they attend the saint, and in the Voyage of Maelduin, an Irish Christian Immram, or voyage tale with pre-Christian roots, there is an Island of the Otter, where the sailors are fed salmon, a symbol of wisdom as already discussed, and showing another otter- salmon relationship. The link with death which can be found with the Afanc and Morfran's possible connections to Brân/ Branwen are also found in the tale of the Irish hero Cúchulainn, who in one version of his tale kills an otter in his dying moments, when he realises it is drinking his blood. As Cúchulainn is under a *geis*, or taboo to never eat the meat of a hound, after which he is called (Cúchulainn means the hound of Culann) striking an otter, or water dog, is another sign of his impending doom and deaths approach.[34]

In this way we can see that Cerridwen becoming an otter is a deeply significant act, bound up with the Otherworld and the liminality of going between land and water, this world and the next, as well as pointing to possible links with earlier death or battle cults, especially when connected to her son/s Morfran / Affagdu, and her earlier shapeshift into a hound to chase Gwion as the hare, as the otter is often known as the water dog. This cult or cults may well have reached far beyond Wales to Ireland and Gaulish Brittany, if we are to connect her tale with the echoes found elsewhere. Dogs in turn, as already discussed have these underworld / Otherworld associations which are doubly underlined at this stage.

Exercise: Otter Swimming

Give yourself 20 minutes uninterrupted time for this exercise. Create a safe and comfortable sacred space, in whichever way you prefer, and light a central candle in honour of Cerridwen, as described earlier.

Take three deep breaths for water, three for air and three for land, and close your eyes or let your vision rest gently upon the candle flame.

Let your outer awareness fade, and using your inner vision see yourself seated at the edge of the river watching the water rushing by below you. The light is dim, it will soon be dawn, but you can see well enough to watch the water flow past you and make out the fresh green of the grassy bank on which you sit. Let yourself breathe and take this in for a while, in your inner ear hear the chatter of the river as it makes it way downstream, you hear voices and laughter and music within its ever-changing tones and rhythms.

After a while, ask the river to bring to you an otter guide, that you may swim together and learn the wisdom of the otter. Look out over the water as a trail of bubbles comes your way and a bright sleek otter breaks the surface and mounts the bank beside you. its fur is wet and smooth, its eyes are bright and dark, its teeth are white and very sharp. It sits opposite you in silence for a moment and you greet it, asking for its friendship and wisdom. Look deeply into its eyes.

Gradually, you look down at your own hands and feet and see that for a short time, you have changed, and become kin with the otter, with your own paws and claws and sleek damp fur. Spend a while listening to the river with your new otter ears. See around you in the patterns of the water with your new otter eyes.

Follow the otter, whether it guides you across land or into the river, as it hunts and plays according to its nature. Every act in the Otherworld, every moment in communion with another being is its own tuition and blessing, so let this time unfold as it will. It is its own treasure.

After a while you will be led back to the river bank. Give your thanks to the otter spirit and gently see your hands and feet returning to their human form, your body and spirit back and whole as it was before and is every day.

Thank the river, and using your breath, let the vision fade, and your spirit return to the room in which your body sits. Wiggle your toes and shake out your arms and hands to feel yourself back into your body. Close your sacred space and extinguish your candle, thanking Cerridwen for her tuition. Take some time to eat and drink to fully ground yourself back in the present, and record your experiences in your journal if you wish.

Bird (Welsh: Aderyn)

In the next stage of the tale, Gwion / Taliesin turns into a bird, "yn ederyn ir wybr" (into a bird in the air) to escape Cerridwen-as-otter. Here we have the transition from the realm of water to the realm of sky, completing the sacred triad of earth sea and sky found within the Welsh bardic tradition. The realm of air is usually understood as being related to ideas about thought and inspiration, youth and the early part of the day, as well as being the realm of the gods and stellar energies or beings. Certainly, the Celts and the early Britons once had an extensive body of star lore, traces of which can still be found in some Welsh myths such as those relating to Arianrhod in the *Mabinogi* – Caer Arianrhod was the Welsh name for the Corona Borealis. The sky is seen as a place of expansive overview and a greater perspective.

The original source texts don't say which bird Gwion / Taliesin turns into but given that Cerridwen is said to turn into a hawk in response to pursue him, it seems that Gwion / Taliesin would most likely have turned into either a wren or a raven. Wrens and ravens both have a significant position in Welsh / Brythonic myth, as do hawks, owls and eagles, but given that Cerridwen as hawk pursues him it seems we could eliminate owls, as night birds, and eagles as not being natural prey to a hawk.

The wren is called *dryw* in Welsh, which related to the Welsh word for druid, Derwydd. Considered a bird of cunning and cleverness, it is considered the king of the birds despite its small size. There is a story about how it became king following a competition about which bird could fly the highest. The eagle was confident it could win the competition as no one could fly higher, but the tiny wren sat on its back and when the eagle reached the highest it could go, the wren leapt of his back and flew high still thus winning his crown. This could make the wren seem like a trickster bird, reminiscent perhaps of the tricksy character of the wizard / druid Gwydion, but it could equally be said to teach about the importance of utilizing everything around you and the skills of others to achieve your ends – put to good use that could be a very druid like quality, as they were known as peacemakers, judges and diplomats who could unite tribes to a common cause, as well as for their magical and bardic skills. A wren would therefore be a very suitable bird to transform into as part of a bardic initiation.

The raven or crow, however, also has a strong likelihood here. Ravens and crows are associated with war and death, as travellers to the realms beyond and with the voice of prophecy. Two very important figures in Welsh / Brythonic myth are connected to the raven – Brân and Branwen, whose names mean raven, and white raven. The raven is also perhaps closely related to Cerridwen's son, Morfran, the great crow, or the sea raven. Knowing how the tale develops we can see that Gwion is in the process of becoming Taliesin, Cerridwen's son, himself, and this together with the raven's association with prophecy seem relevant here. In Ireland, the raven is associated with the Morrigan who is a goddess of sovereignty, war and death, and she is known to utter prophecy throughout her tales. Brân also becomes a speaker of prophecy when he dies and asks that his head be cut off that it can continue to advise and entertain his comrades. Brân also asks eventually that his head be placed in Tower hill in London, so that it can watch over the land from the seat of sovereignty. Ravens are highly intelligent birds and are still kept at the tower of London to this day – it is said that if they ever leave then the Isle of Britain will be in great peril. They are also eaters of carrion, consuming the dead which leads to their association with the underworld. This is all very reminiscent of the river goddess Aerwen 'renowned in carnage' 'spreader of battle' who resides in the Afon Dyfrdwy, (river Dee) which flows into Llyn Tegid. Ravens and hawks are known for their arial battles, and a flock of ravens or crows will often all attack a single hawk in defence of their territory and their young which the larger hawk is able to predate with relative ease if it goes unchallenged. The obvious power and enmity between these two birds is palpable to anyone who has ever seen the spectacle of their battles, and it seems likely therefore that the bird form that Gwion / Taliesin chose would be the raven, which suits the darker underbelly of the tale and its half-forgotten warrior aspects.

Exercise: Wren or Raven?

It could be that the tale deliberately fails to mention which bird form Gwion chose, so that different aspects could be drawn from the tale at different occasions, or that which bird it was has changed over time. Certainly, this presents a place where two different strands of learning and inner development can be explored. One the wit and cunning of the diplomatic druids, with the wren, the other being the Otherworld travelling prophecy uttering raven, with its reputation steeped in the blood of warriors and the journey between life and death.

Which aspect calls to you the most? And why? Give yourself 10 minutes or more, to feel into which bird you would choose, which calls to you the most.

Exercise: Flying with the Raven, Flying with the Wren

Give yourself 20 minutes uninterrupted time for this exercise. Create a safe and comfortable sacred space, in whichever way you prefer, and light a central candle for in honour of Cerridwen, as described earlier.

Take three deep breaths for water, three for air and three for land, and close your eyes or let your vision rest gently upon the candle flame.

Let your outer awareness fade, and using your inner vision see yourself seated by the riverbank, looking up into a deep blue sky. Let the chatter of the water fill your ears, its laughter and rumbles and see if you can sense the wind blowing the trees around you, mussing your hair, and shushing in the leaves like the sound of the sea. Let yourself be with this scene for a time, breathing and building your feeling of connection to this sacred place.

When you are ready, call out to the sky to bring you a guide, you may decide to ask for a raven guide, or a wren, or see what type of bird arrives for you. It may be different every time you repeat this exercise, or the same each time, at least for a while. Watch as the shape of a bird comes to you across the sky and lands near you. It sits opposite you in silence for a moment and you greet it, asking for its friendship and wisdom. Look deeply into its eyes. Study it carefully, and ask what it could teach you. You might like to ask about its place in the tale. After a while it begins to fly around you and you sense a change within you, as your arms change to wings and your form becomes the same as you guide. Easy as air you lift into the sky and fly with it, arcing high in the sky and low over the water, ecstatic and alive to your own flight and the endless horizons around you. Follow the bird spirit wherever it leads you. Every act in the Otherworld, every moment in communion with another being is its own tuition and blessing, so let this time unfold as it will. It is its own treasure.

After a while you will be led back to the river bank. Give your thanks to the bird spirit and gently see your hands and feet returning to their human form, your body and spirit back and whole as it was before and is every day.

Thank the sky, and using your breath, let the vision fade, and your spirit return to the room in which your body sits. Wiggle your toes and shake out your arms and hands to feel yourself back into your body. Close your sacred space and extinguish your candle, thanking Cerridwen for her tuition. Take some time to eat and drink to fully ground yourself back in the present, and record your experiences in your journal if you wish.

Hawk (Welsh: Gwalch)

Just as Gwion/ Taliesin turns into a bird, Cerridwen turns *yn walch*, 'into a hawk' in her pursuit of him. A hawk is generally a generic term for a host of different raptors in the Accipitridae family. They are master predators of the sky, a position it shares with the eagle, the only bird it will come second to as an aerial hunter. For this reason, hawks were popular hunting birds in the Medieval period. Falconry was an almost entirely aristocratic leisure pursuit with a series of strict and formal rules about who could hunt with what type of hawk at the court. Buzzards, Sparrowhawks, Kestrels and increasingly the impressive and distinctive Red Kite are still to be found in Wales, although sadly eagles have long gone (there are plans currently to reintroduce them). Known for flying high and for their keen sight, hawks like their larger counterparts the eagle, reach places in the sky that other birds find hard to access, and anyone watching a hawk in flight, especially when hunting can be astonished and deeply moved by how it can hover in the air, tracking its prey far below. Just at the right moment, the hawk will descend and snatch its prey – often a hare or a rabbit, but sometimes other birds and chicks from the nest, with its sharp claws, and arc off across the sky with its prey still squirming beneath it locked in its grasp with no hope of escape.

Hawks don't feature as strongly in Welsh folklore as eagles do, although they are mentioned here and there, most notably in the figure of *Gwalchmai*, and old name for the Arthurian knight, Gawain. *Gwalchmai* means 'hawk of the May'. In modern Druidry hawks are connected to the element of air, and the direction of the east, as the start of the day and the early part of the year and the cycle of life – connecting it with youthly vigour – a suitable association for Gawain. While the term Gwalchmai may be a borrowing from Breton retellings of the Arthurian myths, there is a town in Anglesey called Gwalchmai and there was a 12th Century Welsh poet based on Anglesey called *Gwalchmai ap Meilyr* – one of the Gogynfeirdd ('less early poets') who served the princes, as opposed to the *Cynfeirdd* ('the early poets') such as Taliesin. Gwalchmai ap Meilyr and the name of the village are perhaps a sign of the popularity of this image, the Hawk of May, as well as the popularity of the Arthurian tales. In some ways the hawk is seen perhaps as a symbol of wisdom in the wild, of natural nobility and cold keenness of vision – similar to that of the eagle. The eagle (eryr) appears in several notable places in Welsh mythology and medieval literature – in the tale of Culhwch and Olwen one of the oldest of birds, is the eagle of Gwernabwy, and the doomed son of Arianrhod Llew Llaw Gyffes is turned into a rotting eagle – a symbol of royalty and power gone awry and poisoned – after Gronw slays him. The vast national park of Eryri – the place of the eagles – also known by its English name Snowdonia shows the national importance of this most majestic of birds. However, the eagle never seems to be seen as a female in the old stories, suggesting perhaps that in the time of recording written versions of *Ystoria* and *Hanes Taliesin* from the oral sources, a hawk was seemed to be a more suitable bird for Cerridwen, a trifle tamer for a woman and a witch at that. We may never know.

Exercise: Flying with the Hawk

Give yourself 20 minutes uninterrupted time for this exercise. Create a safe and comfortable sacred space, in whichever way you prefer, and light a central candle in honour of Cerridwen, as described earlier.

Take three deep breaths for water, three for air and three for land, and close your eyes or let your vision rest gently upon the candle flame.

Let your outer awareness fade, and using your inner vision see yourself seated at the edge of the river looking up into a deep blue sky. Let the chatter of the water fill your ears, its laughter and rumbles and see if you can sense the wind blowing the trees around you, mussing your hair, and shushing in the leaves like the sound of the sea. Let yourself be with this scene for a time, breathing and building your feeling of connection to this sacred place.

When you are ready, call out to the sky to bring you a hawk guide. See it arcing through the sky high above, hovering on the wind and then darting straight and fast as an arrow towards you, its bright eye fixed upon you from afar. With talons as sharp and golden as a druid's sickle, it grasps you by the shoulders and bears you up into the sky. The land falls away beneath you into a vast green patchwork of forests and fields and rolling hills, the river a silver thread woven through it and glinting in the sun. Soon the fields and forest turn to rugged craggy hills and mountains touched purple and bronze with heather and through the vasty blue of the sky you see the silver grey of the sea edging your view to the furthest west. You feel your heart yearn towards the horizon, and become aware that the hawk no longer carries you like its prey, but that the two of you soar through the skies together – feel the stretch of your wings, the light caress of the air in your feathers, the sun glinting in your golden eyes as if you are made all of air and light. Fly with your hawk guide, let them show you what you need to see and learn and feel from this experience. Look down at the world below you, the hillsides a tumble of precious emeralds and amethysts, the fierce heart within you beating to the rhythm of the heart of the world, all the life blood beating in the chests of the land creatures beneath you seem slow to the mighty presence you feel. Up here see how your perspective changes, feel the fierce joy of your freedom, feather light and sharp as steel.

After a while you will be led back to the river and the soft grassy bank. Give your thanks to the hawk spirit and gently see your hands and feet returning to their human form; your body and spirit back and whole as it was before and is every day.

Thank the sky, and using your breath, let the vision fade, and your spirit return to the room in which your body sits. Wiggle your toes and shake out your arms and hands to feel yourself back into your body. Close your sacred space and extinguish your candle, thanking Cerridwen for her tuition. Take some time to eat and drink to fully ground yourself back in the present, and record your experiences in your journal if you wish.

Grain and Hen

The final stages of the sacred chase are when Gwion turns himself into a piece of grain, a tiny seed hidden among others. This is a fascinating and powerful symbol, a tiny thing, easily over looked and yet it is the starting point, the miniscule super-condensed potential that contains all life springing from it, waiting to be released in the right conditions. A seed is a powerful thing, a provider of life in that it can give sustenance, as well as the place in which life resides almost before it becomes life… a place of ultimate beginning. In this way Gwion becomes proto-enlightened, the very stage before a rebirth, for he has not come to this place unwittingly but of his own choice, as a result of the transformations and challenges he has already been through in his pursuit by Cerridwen, and in his initiation through and within the Awen itself. This is the very depths of the cauldron, the place of death, where any life and personality, any sense of self is extinguished. Unlike a hare, or a salmon, or a bird, a seed is a thing, and object more than a living creation despite the fact that so much potential life resides within it. It is inanimate, without agency, in a sense it is earth itself in that life may come from it but it is not 'alive' – yet. In his transformations Gwion has become a creature of the land, the hare, the water, the salmon, and the sky, the wren or the raven... Now he has completed this sacred triplicity he has come to a still, passive place where he is both a singular point, a bead on the thread of life, and also at one with it all – where all potential creation is within him.

Along comes Cerridwen, not as hound, or otter, or hawk, not as the predator, but as something domestic, a hybrid of land and sky, of wild forest and homely farmyard, the hen. A close look at a red hen will show you this is a bird of great beauty, of shimmering colours and a wild ferocity in their eyes, a brutal sharpness in the claws... yet this is also the humble hen, the creature kept by every cottage and castle alike. In terms of lore, it is a great leveller, a creature known and accessible to all, who is kept either for food or the eggs they produce, eggs, of course, being an ancient symbol for the soul. This is a humble position for Cerridwen to choose, yet one which holds all within it – her chase has taken her from wild river to mountain top to the yard of the cottage, where at last, she consumes Gwion-as-grain and becomes pregnant with him. Again, Gwion is in a state of potential but here has gone from mute object, from the place of death in life, into life itself, into living baby in the womb of the goddess. Here at least he may gain further insights and knowledge, here is the place of initiation itself, from death to life again, held in the blackness of the cauldron as womb.

Finally, after nine months, Cerridwen births Gwion as her own son, and is struck by his beauty and the love she feels for him. Her anger and need for retribution have passed, her tests and challenges are complete and now, holding this sacred baby in her arms, we are reminded again, that Cerridwen is the fierce mother, who births wisdom and great power within those she chooses. Yet Gwion's journey cannot end here, in this place of myth, instead he must carry what he has learnt into the world, and there is more initiation to come, for this is his second birth, first as Gwion and now as the child of Cerridwen, he has been birthed twice out of three. Before his transformation into Taliesin is complete, he needs at last to become one with all things, and with this Cerridwen wraps him and places him in a leather bag – another womb, or sometimes a small coracle, and sets him out upon the sea, to return in time, to the mortal world.

Exercise: The Seed Within and the Kernel of Wisdom

Give yourself 20 minutes uninterrupted time for this exercise. Create a safe and comfortable sacred space, in which ever why you prefer, and light a central candle for in honour of Cerridwen, as described earlier.

Take three deep breaths for water, three for air and three for land, and close your eyes or let your vision rest gently upon the candle flame.

Let your outer awareness fade, and using your inner vision see yourself standing by the river's edge, with the hills and the mountains in the distance, and the lake in the valley below. A little way off you see a small cottage, with a thatched roof and an open yard around it with animal pens and a small barn to the side. You take a moment to feel all that you have been so far, hare and hound, salmon and otter, raven or wren, and hawk and you feel the wild land in your bones, the wilderness in your eye. The small domestic scene in front of you seems strange and simple compared to the feel of the wind in your feathers, but it brings a memory with it, of home and your daily life, a life of smaller simpler things from before your transformations. You approach the cottage and the barn, feeling a great presence coming fast behind you on your heals, and as you move you become aware of your heart beating hard in your chest, pushing your forward to evade what hunts you. You dive into the barn, a place of shadows and with every step you find to your amazement that you are growing smaller and smaller, aware only now of the beating of your heart, you distil down and down your body fading to nothing until you become the single point focus of you heart, beating... you become aware of yourself as a single bead of light, a seed of potential, with all life within it enclosed in the darkness. The beating slows and pauses.

With sharp suddenness, you feel yourself lifted up and the darkness becomes complete around you as you find yourself falling down and down further into the great cauldron – whether this be by the lakeside or in the body of Cerridwen herself you cannot tell for they are one and the same.

You descend in darkness for what seems like an age, silence and stillness roaring within you like the sound of the distant sea. At last, you cease and find a place of rest. Stay here a while, surrounded by the great giver of life and death, at the place where they are the same.

After a while you become aware of the beating of your heart again, its rhythm finally and steadily increasing, and the light that you are grows, radiating outwards and illuminating all around you. You find yourself growing and rising, until at last you break out into the light.

This is your soul reborn, your second birth.

Cerridwen is holding you safe and steady in her smooth and ancient hands, she smiles upon you with the light you are shining in her eyes, which are as young as the dawn. She breaths a blessing upon you, and sets you in a coracle, upon the gentle seas of the morning, the place where all mortal memory and learning and being becomes one, to find your way on the currents of life, and in time, to bring your gifts back to the mortal, everyday world.

Exercise: Adrift on the Sea of Unbeing

Cerridwen sets Taliesin adrift upon the sea, some versions say in a coracle, others in a leather bag – either way we see here that the initiate is held in the womb again, this time upon the ocean, to let his fate or destiny lead him where it will. For a while at least Taliesin is in a place with no forms, at one with the depths of Annwfn – the deep place, in its most primal form, much as a baby in the womb. unseen and unknowable.

The sea here is, like the cauldron, something that can be seen to hold all life, and yet it is also a place out of time, away from world. In some ways it can be seen as the outer reaches of the spirit world, or perhaps more accurately, the most inner place – where divisions and boundaries break down and all things become one.

Perform this exercise when you have several hours free. Create a darkened space, and perhaps get yourself a recording of ocean sounds, and allow yourself to enter into a deep meditative space without any focus, lying back somewhere comfortable with the only sounds being the ocean, the sighing breath of the sea around you. Let your tensions and any conscious thoughts float away, with no agenda. Set no time limit, and have no aim in mind other than to enter into this state of unbeing, un-doing…breathe slow and deep, sleep and dream if that is what comes.

Allowing the mind and the spirit to rest in this way is vital for our wellbeing and for rebalancing after any psychic or spirit work. You may find sudden flashes of ideas or messages come to you, equally you may find they come to you later, now that you have given your mind enough space in which to receive them. In time, you will naturally come back to a place of stirring when it is time to return to your day and normal activity, but allow yourself to come back here, often, whenever you find yourself in need of clearer vision or renewal. You may find such times offer you far greater insights than you at first imagine.

When you return and apply your magic and knowledge in the mortal world, when you have walked this initiatory path enough to draw wisdom from the Otherworld to apply here and now, then and only then are you born again by your deeds, a third and final time, fully integrated back into life. An initiate.

The chase

Endnotes

1 Manuscript: National Library of Wales (NLW MS 1553A).

2 Manuscript: (Peniarth MS 111, RMW II, ii, 664-71).

3 Manuscript: National Library of Wales (NLW MS5276D).

4 Manuscript: National Library of Wales (NLW MS6209E).

5 Manuscript: (Panton MS 55, RWM II, iii, 861-2).

6 Manuscript: National Library of Wales (NLW MS 13100B / NLW MS 2005B).

7 Nennius is unlikely to have been the compiler of *Historia Brittonum* with his name only becoming attached to the text in the mid-11th Century – thus the text is now considered to

be a product of the 'Nennian tradition' rather than by him, yet the piece is still called Nennius's Historia Brittonum for general convenience and clarity.

8   P. K. Ford, *Ystoria Taliesin*, 1992, University of Wales Press, Cardiff. p 1.

9   P. K. Ford, 1992, p 35.

10 M. Haycock, 2015 p321.

11 M. Haycock, 2015, p 320.

12 L. Thorpe, (trans) Gerald of Wales, *The Journey through Wales and the Description of Wales* Penguin classics 2004. Kindle Edition. p246 location 3409.

13 M. Haycock, 2015, pp. 318-20.

14 M. Haycock, 2015, p. 322.

15 M. Haycock, 2015, p110.

16 R. Bromwich (trans) John Jones, Gellilyfdy NLW Peniarth 111 (c. 1607) pp1ff, found in *Trioedd Ynys Prydein: The Triads of the Island of Britain,* University of Wales Press, 2017, p452.

17 I. Williams, *Chwedl Taliesin*, University of Wales, Board of Celtic Studies, Cardiff. 1957. p.4.

18 M. Haycock, 2015, p320.

19 S. Baring-Gould, and J. Fisher, *The Lives of the British Saints: The Saints of Wales and Cornwall and Such Irish Saints as Have Dedications in Britain,* Volume 2, (C. J. Clark, 1908). p 9.

20 E, Davies, *The Mythology and Rites of the British Druids,* J. Booth, London, 1909. p 205 https://archive.org/details/mythologyritesof00davirich/page/204/mode/2up?view=theater&q=creirwy

21 R. Bromwich, 2017. P 451.

22 John Jones, *Hanes Taliesin,* in P. K. Ford, 1992. P132-3.

23 https://www.etymonline.com/word/Gwendolyn#etymonline_v_14404 accessed 9/6/23

24 I.L. Foster, 'Gwynn ap Nudd', in *Duanaire Finn,* iii, ed. Gerard Murphy, Irish Texts Society, no. 43 (Dublin, 1953), 198–205.

25   Myths and Legends of Bala, http://www.llangollenmuseum.
     org.uk/MythsAndLegends/UpperDeeValley/LlynTegid.
     htm <accessed 9/6/23.>

26   With thanks to Dr Simon Rodway at University of
     Aberystwyth for his assistance here.

27   Pitcairn, Robert (1833), Ancient Criminal Trials in Scotland,
     vol. 3, part 2, Bannatyne Club. p. 607.

28   See "The Dialogue of Gwyddno Garanhir and Gwyn ap
     Nudd, The Black Book of Carmarthen" XXXIII, J. Rowland,
     Early Welsh Saga Poetry: A study and Edition of the Englynion,
     D.S. Brewer, 1990. P506-7.

29   Also known as Aerwen and Ayrwen, 'woman of slaughter'
     or 'Slaughter goddess'.

30   Annwn (ann-oon) was originally spelled Annwfn (ann-ow-
     ven).

31   As discussed earlier, as a recurring motif, the links between
     Mabon, Taliesin (and Pryderi) hint at earlier tradition.

32   Mabon is imprisoned at Caerloyw (Gloucester). The
     Mabinogion, trans, Sioned Davies, (oxford world classics,
     2007. P. 330, 402, et al.

33   J. Koch, *Celtic Culture - A Historical Encyclopaedia*, A B C C L
     I O, 2006. P. 19.

34   J. Koch, *Celtic Culture - A Historical Encyclopaedia*, A B C C L
     I O, 2006. P 508.

Part 3

Cerridwen in Context

Cerridwen and Annwfn
A Goddess Beyond Time and Space

The Welsh spirit realm, or Otherworld, is known as Annwfn (also known by its later name Annwn), meaning 'The deep place'. This is, despite its term as the Otherworld, not separate from this world but could perhaps be understood as another layer of existence, somewhere that resembles this world but is accessed either via a liminal point on the landscape or via a shift in consciousness, perhaps to a 'deeper' level of awareness. This is where the Awen can most readily be accessed and connection with Cerridwen be most fruitfully achieved. On one level the story of Cerridwen and Taliesin takes place on the physical shores of Llyn Tegid, but to be more accurate we could see this being a tale that takes place perennially, out of time, in Annwfn. From here Taliesin undergoes his transformations experiencing deeper and other aspects of Annwfn, especially during his long sojourn out at sea, before finally re-entering the mortal world when he is found at the weir by Elphin.

By undergoing his initiation with Cerridwen, and tasting her brew, Taliesin received the Awen, which in his case is magical and visionary knowledge which make him both an inspired bard, but also one who is able to speak with the voice of spirit – he has gained access to a realm beyond time and space and is able to assimilate and use the sum of *all* knowledge. This means in modern understanding, that he is able to access the knowledge of his many lives and indeed of experience between lives, not only his own, but of all creation. He learns by his shapeshifting, and his time in Cerridwen's womb as well as out to sea, what it is to be *all* things – he has accessed a transcendent space and uses that experience to bring wisdom back to the mortal world.

The Transmigration of Souls

The Celtic belief in reincarnation and the transmigration of souls seems to be solidly attested in the writings of Caesar. In his *De Bello Gallico*, he writes that in the views of the Celts and druids, "souls do not become extinct, but pass after death from one body to another, and they think that men by this tenet are in a great degree excited to valour, the fear of death being disregarded."[1] Here we see this idea has continued and perhaps evolved in the Taliesin tradition not as a source of valour for warriors but as a way to gain wisdom and magical skill. Elis Gruffydd relates a belief in Wales that illustrates this idea of many lives in relation to Taliesin. In his Chronicle, Gruffydd states that not only did Taliesin have other lives, but that he had in fact also been that other illustrious figure of myth and legend, Merlin, (Myrddin) whose abilities also had supernatural origins. Functioning much like a Buddha, Christ or other ascended or supernatural figure who descends to assist the mortal world where he had specific tasks before returning to his home in Annwfn.

Some people hold to the opinion and maintain firmly that Merlin was a spirit in human form, who was in that shape from the time of Vortigern until the beginning of King

Arthur's time when he disappeared. After that, this spirit appeared again in the time of Maelgwn Gwynedd at which time he is called Taliesin, who is said to be alive yet in a place called Caer Sidia. Thence he appeared a third time in the days of Merfyn Frych son of Esyllt, whose son he was said to be, and in this period, he was called Merlin the mad. From that day to this, he is said to be resting in Caer Sidia (Caer Sidi) whence certain people believe firmly that he will rise up once again before doomsday.[2]

Here we see how in Medieval Wales the idea of an archetypal poet, embodying the spirit of divinely inspired wisdom was well established, and it is but a small step from here to see Taliesin as a divine figure in his own right. That Taliesin holds both a divine / spirit form and remains a historical person makes sense in this context as the court bards were at once both flesh and blood people, as well as a divinely inspired and even frenzied, ecstatic practitioners of verbal ritual who embodied beings from the Otherworld and transmitted the knowledge they found there, much as we would understand a shaman or a medium would today, although in a specifically Welsh/ Brythonic context and within the constraints of Bardic ritual performance.

The Awenyddion
Welsh bards were not the only practitioners who drew their wisdom and abilities from Annwfn. In the Welsh and wider Celtic traditions, we also find the Otherworld as a source of healing and herbal knowledge. There are many examples of this, but a famous one can be seen in the famous physicians of the Myddfai who claimed they literally drew their skill from the mother of their family who was a woman of Annwfn, arising from a lake to which she later returned. We also have the figure of the Awenyddion, a type of soothsayer recorded in Giraldus Cambrensis' s *Description of Wales*;

There are certain persons in Cambria, whom you will find nowhere else, called Awenyddion, or people inspired; when consulted upon any doubtful event, they roar out violently, are rendered beside themselves, and become, as it were, possessed by a spirit. They do not deliver the answer to what is required in a connected manner; but the person who skilfully observes them, will find, after many preambles, and many nugatory and incoherent, though ornamented speeches, the desired explanation conveyed in some turn of a word: they are then roused from their ecstasy, as from a deep sleep, and, as it were, by violence compelled to return to their proper senses. After having answered the questions, they do not recover till violently shaken by other people; nor can they remember the replies they have given. If consulted a second or third time upon the same point, they will make use of expressions totally different; perhaps they speak by the means of fanatic and ignorant spirits. These gifts are usually conferred upon them in dreams: some seem to have sweet milk or honey poured on their lips; others fancy that a written schedule is applied to their mouths and on awaking they publicly declare that they have received this gift.[3]

Here we see the Awenyddion is conveying answers and prophecy via possession by a spirit, where they appear to be in a kind of trance or ecstatic fit. Cambrensis also states that they appear to receive this ability whilst in a dream – but the source of this knowledge, drawn from the Awen and by extension from Annwfn is clear. Elsewhere in Scotland and Ireland, magical, healing and prophetic or divinatory skill are also gained from the Otherworld, especially by those practitioners known as Cunning folk or fairy doctors, who were often said to have been given their gifts from specific fairies or Otherworldly beings. Here in Wales, however, we see that this process is overseen extensively by Cerridwen, who acts as initiator and mediator between this world and Annwfn, or as a divine muse drawing mortal consciousness into the deeper place of altered and visionary consciousness.

Awen and Sovereignty

Access to Annwfn was not only used by bards and magical practitioners, however, as already mentioned – it was also used to gain legitimacy for leaders, as can be seen in the first branch of the *Mabinogi*, where Pwyll becomes a wise leader via his friendship with Arawn, a king of Annwfn[4] – in this sense the Awen, as a divine breath or wind from Annwfn brings correct conduct and enforces heroic ideals as well as the wisdom to discern what these are and recognise them in action – a key skill in the role of the court bard when honouring his lord. Annwfn also confers leadership in the form of the figure of sovereignty, usually in the form of a woman from the Otherworld who marries the king and legitimises or improves his authority – as can be seen in the stories of Pwyll and Rhiannon, as well as Arthur and Guinevere / Gwenhwyfar (the white spirit or fairy).[5] To have access to Annwfn's divine wisdom be controlled and mediated by an Otherworldly woman is a common motif, but in the case of Cerridwen we may see she is not only reminiscent of some other figures from Welsh and Irish medieval literature but also perhaps to pre-Christian figures also, as in the goddess seen on the Gundestrup cauldron conveying ritual transformation upon a series of warriors via submersion in her cauldron. In this sense we may see Cerridwen as the latest face or iteration of a goddess who goes back very far indeed – from Cerridwen to Aerwen perhaps, and further back into Celtic pre-history.

Bardic Initiation – Seeking Awen

Initiation and the seeking if inner vision has a long history in Britain and Ireland, often with the seeker performing vigils in nature or as in the case of the Scottish bards and the Irish

Fili, seeking inspiration via sensory deprivation in complete darkness. The Irish bards would make offerings, before closing themselves inside a darkened roundhouse, where they lay with their hands over their eyes for sometimes days, until inspiration and illumination came upon them. There are numerous hints in the Welsh traditions that something similar was performed by the Welsh bards – we know from folklore that the mountain Cadair Idris was used and still is – as a place to seek visions. Those who stayed overnight on its summit were said to return dead, mad or a poet... Immersion in the wilderness has long been used to seek wisdom and it could also be that in the distant past rituals, potentially entheogenic ones, were also performed, much like Cerridwen and her visionary brew, high in the mountains away from prying eyes and the everyday world.

Another possibility is that the Welsh bards utilised ritual burial, or perhaps performed vigils in other darkened spaces in order to receive their Awen. The famous bard, Aneurin, refers perhaps to ritual burial in order to receive the Awen in his epic poem the Gododdin.

I'm no weary lord,
I avenge no affront,
I laugh no laughter,
Under crawlers' feet,
Outstretched my knee
In an earthen dwelling,
A chain of iron
Around my two knees...
I, not I, Aneirin,
Taliesin knows it,
Skilled in word-craft,
Sang the Gododdin
Before the day dawned.[6]

Here we see the poet Aneirin, lays "outstretched...in an earthen dwelling" perhaps ritually bound, with crawling insects overhead, suggesting he is underground or under earth. Another interesting part of this poem is the line "I, not I, Aneirin" suggesting he is both himself and not himself – the poet ritually embodying the spirit of the bard or other Otherworldly intelligence. He gains his poetic inspiration overnight, and "Sang to Gododdin, before the day dawned". The line "Taliesin knows it" shows us that this practice was one shared with Taliesin or those who worked in that tradition.

Another example suggesting ritual burial or restraint with a resultant series of inner visions can be found in the work of Taliesin himself, in the poem Kat Godeu, 'the battle of the trees'.

I was in a multitude of forms
Before I was unfettered:
I was a slender mottled sword
Made from the hand
I was a droplet in the air
I was the stellar radiance of the stars...[7]

Folklore also hints at the ritual practices of the Taliesin tradition and by extension, the Cerridwen tradition. The folklorist W.Y. Evans-Wentz informs us that cairns and barrow mounds were sometimes known as 'the womb or court of Cerridwen' and were believed to be places of druid inititation[8] and there is a small burial cairn, dating to the Bronze age, known as Bedd Taliesin,[9] or the grave of Taliesin, in Ceredigion, above the small town of Taliesin. A series of waterfalls and pools in the area may also, like Llyn Tegid, have once had a ritual purpose as initiatory cauldrons in the Taliesin tradition. While it may never be known for certain that these places formed ritual sites in the bardic traditions, it seems very likely.

Cauldrons in the Celtic Traditions

The image of the cauldron holds special power in the Celtic traditions of Ireland and Wales, and its presence as a magical ritual object as well as a practical one is well attested throughout the archaeological record of Celtic northern Europe. Cauldrons varied in the Iron Age and later from simple cooking vessels to large elaborate objects of status, capable of serving large numbers of people – what was held within them naturally varies but those of high status appear to mostly have been used to hold some form of brewed liquid rather than food, and those with particular ritual significance may well have been used to hold entheogenic brews and magical potions for a whole host of aims.

Many things can go into a cauldron, and indeed if it serves as a cooking pot or potion maker, it will hold may ingredients. We are told in the story that Cerridwen was so busy gathering ingredients for her potion that she needed assistants to stir it and keep the fire fed. So, it is when vision seeking, and in the pursuit of the spiritual life within the Celtic traditions, where what is included, rather than what is excluded, and how we expand our awareness and the generosity of our spirits, rather than narrow it down, that provides the illumination we seek. This is not to say that discernment isn't important – it surely is! But while a minimalist approach may be desired in much of eastern philosophy, in the Celtic traditions generally we see that spiritual wisdom is gained by expansion rather than narrowing the mind down to a single point, by a sensual appreciation of the nature and the wisdom of the body – our humanity with its faults and perfections is the model for an enlightened being, one who is humbled by the wisdom and compassion of the heart and the human condition as well as the discipline of the mind and body is our guide for honourable, and wise conduct and by extension, what is required for us to be fit vessels for the Awen and in close connection with Annwfn.

When we think of a cauldron, immediately we sense that this is a communal object – an object that serves more than one person, capable of providing for a whole family or gathering in one sitting – while the materials to make a cauldron may vary from clay or iron to elaborate silver or bronze, still the thing itself seems by nature egalitarian, providing for all. There is status and power in its generosity, in its attitude of service, in a way that is the absolute opposite of other iron age and Celtic treasures we may be aware of, such as weapons or shields. The cauldron by its nature is a holding presence, its action as it is heated is that of transformation, of alchemical mystery, it holds secrets and tantalising suggestions within it. Some modern scholars and goddess worshippers see the cauldron as an instinctively feminine object, reminiscent of the womb, and it is likely that this imagery and significance was not missed by the Celtic ritualists of the past, as such it also holds the opposite symbolism, that of the tomb, the open grave, the dolmen arch into the burial mound or the ritual grain pit with its crouched burial deep within it to propitiate the land.

The Gundestrup Cauldron

This dual nature of the cauldron can be seen especially strikingly in the most famous cauldron in the archaeological record – the Gundestrup cauldron, which we have discussed several times already. Named after the bog in Denmark in which it was found, having been ritually deposited as an offering somewhere between 200 BCE and 100 CE. This silver cauldron would have been immensely valuable, and had been ritually dismantled when it was buried. When it was rediscovered in 1891 most but not all of the pieces were found, allowing only a partial reconstruction. Upon its sides, and in a style quite different to that found in Denmark, there are elephants, lions as well as other animals and the depictions of several unknown gods – although the imagery does give us some clues as to identifying them some questions regarding the cauldron will never be answered fully. Some of the gods presented are clearly associated with fertility and beauty, while others appear connected to death and warfare, with the more complex scenes depicted on the inside of the cauldron – suggesting perhaps a secret initiatory wisdom, visible only to those who could look within, or perhaps even to illustrate the differences of life on the outside of the cauldron in the normal world – and that of what happens when you go through it, in a symbolic or ritual sense.

The panels of the cauldron all depict scenes with tantalizing suggestions of long forgotten Celtic myth, and even some traces of familiar tales and figures, such as the antlered man thought to be the god Cernunnos, and on the lower half of interior plate E, we see a line of warriors bearing spears and shields, together with a boar-crested helmet. In front of this group is a dog. Dogs are often considered to be guardians of the Otherworld, and behind the dog, there is a figure over twice the size of the others – most likely suggesting that this is a goddess, although the gender is unclear. This deity holds a man upside down, and is about to immerse him in a cauldron. On the upper half of the panel, warriors on horseback with crested helmets and spears ride away to the right, with at the right a horned serpent, sometimes though to be a symbol of regeneration or life force. The two lines are below and above what appears to be a tree, still in leaf, lying sideways. This perhaps suggests what we would now call the world tree, or in Ireland what was the sacred Bile (tree) which served as a mustering point and ritual focus. This scene is often interpreted as depicting fallen warriors being dipped into a cauldron to be reborn into the Otherworld, or being reincarnated in some way. Traces of this idea can be seen in both Irish and Welsh tales, which we shall be turning to next.

Gundestrup cauldron panel – warrior's cauldron goddess

The Cauldron of Brân, the *pair dadeni* (cauldron of rebirth)

Brân the Blessed (Welsh: Bendigeidfran) was a mythological king of Britain. He was a giant, who was known for his good nature. He sought a peace treaty with King Matholwch of Ireland, and as part of his treaty, he gave his sister, Branwen, to Matholwch in marriage. The Irish King and his retinue came to Wales to celebrate and collect Branwen, but Brân's half-brother, Efnysien was jealous and tried to sabotage the marriage and the agreement, by mutilating Matholwch's horses. To assuage the Irish King, Brân gave him a great magic cauldron, which could bring back the dead, in addition to his sister's hand. Matholwch accepted and took Branwen back to Ireland, where she bore a son, Gwern (alder tree). But the Irish did not forget the insult – and treated Branwen poorly. So, she called upon Brân using her magical starlings, and Brân brought his army to Ireland to retrieve her. The Irish suggested they make peace, and build a giant house for Brân, but had a hundred bags, each one hiding a warrior to betray him. Efnysien, however, suspected treachery, and killed all the Irish warriors. Later, again feeling insulted, he murdered Gwern by throwing him into the fire, and another battle breaks out. Seeing that the Irish are using the cauldron to revive their dead warriors, Efnysien hides among the Irish corpses and when he is thrown into the cauldron, he destroys the cauldron from within, sacrificing himself in the process. The Cauldron, the *pair dadeni* had a strange and magical history. It first appeared in Ireland, where it belonged to two giants, *Llassar Llaes Gyfnewid* and his wife *Cymidei Cymeinfoll*, who came from a lake called the lake of the cauldron. Llassar met Matholwch, as he and his wife came from the lake carrying the cauldron. And while he was a giant, his wife Cymidei was twice his size, and she had the ability to give birth every six weeks, and each child was magical so that within six weeks the child would have grown to a fully armed adult warrior. At first Matholwch welcomed the giants, but after they had born hundreds of warriors, the Irish sought to kill them, and built them a house of iron so that they could burn them within it. But the giants escaped, and brought their cauldron with them to Wales, where they sought permission to settle from Brân himself, and thrived in peace.

This cauldron of the giants, with its ability to bring warriors back to life, is deeply reminiscent of the scene depicted on the Gundestrup cauldron, and there is much in this small section of the tale of Brân and Branwen to give us clues to a lost spiritual tradition. Lakes in Celtic tradition are often seen as entry points to and from the Otherworld, or spirit realm, and that the lake is called the lake of the cauldron seems to imply this significance twice over. The lake itself is a cauldron of sorts, a holding and liminal vessel for allowing and mediating access to the Otherworld, and the giant's great size in and of itself are indicators of their Otherworldly status – again this is illustrated in the panel on the Gundestrup cauldron. That Cymidei Cymeinfoll is larger still than her husband seems to add some kind of primeval goddess imagery to the story – and her husband can be seen here as her emissary and representative suggesting perhaps that it is she that has the greater authority.

That she births supernatural warriors at an immense rate is also indicative of her likely divinity as a war goddess or some kind of goddess of life and death – again she appears to be a liminal being with concerns that hinge very much on liminal qualities – in giving birth to warriors it could be said she gives birth to death or death bringers. In this sense like the lake, she is also a cauldron – here functioning as a sacred magical womb, birthing warriors, perhaps as a metaphor for warrior initiation. That she and her husband own a cauldron that will then bring these or other warriors back to life reinforces this imagery and its implications. As well as its ability to bring warriors back from the dead, however, this cauldron also has the peculiar quality that those reanimated from its depths can no longer speak – this lends the warriors another Otherworldly feel but also means they are unable to describe their experience or what they saw as they underwent their transformation. They cannot speak of the Otherworld – this also hints at a now forgotten initiatory tradition, as well as a reminder of the almost universal taboo of interchange between the living and the dead.

The Cauldron of Annwfn

The poem Preiddeu Annwfn (The Spoils of Annwfn) is written in Middle Welsh and is attributed to the bard Taliesin, and possibly written or at least composed as early as the 8th century CE, before finally being recorded in the 14th Century *Book of Taliesin*. It recounts a raid on the Otherworld, Annwfn, by King Arthur to steal the cauldron that resides there. This cauldron, often simply called the cauldron of Annwfn (or its more modern spelling Annwn) is said to be ringed with pearls, and will not boil the meat of a coward. This interesting property is shared with another famous cauldron from the Welsh / Brythonic tradition, that of the Cauldron of the Irishman *Diwrnach*, which is sought as one of the heroic tasks set by the giant *Yspadadden*, in the tale of Culhwch and Olwen. Another staple of the

Brythonic lore is the Middle Welsh tract, *The Thirteen Treasures of the Island of Britain*, which includes the cauldron of Dyrnwch the Giant – probably one and the same character. The idea that this cauldron will not honour cowardliness but will reward bravery is a key detail suggesting an initiatory tradition or the initiatory purpose of the cauldron itself – to imbibe from its depths is an act of bravery. Something similar is seen in yet another cauldron, that of the cauldron or chalice of Manannán mac Lir in the voyage tale *Echtra Cormaic i Tár Tairngiri ocus Ceart Claidib Cormaic* (The adventure of Cormac in Tár Tairngiri and the truth of Cormac's sword). This chalice would break if a lie was said over it and reformed it a truth was said.

The association of cauldrons with honour and initiatory tests is taken a stage further in the Irish Fiannaíocht (Find Cycle) tale *Creach na Teamhrach* (The raid on Tara/Teamhair), where the King of Ireland, Cormac mac Airt, is made by Faelán mac Finn to *go fo ghabhail an choire* (under the fork of a cauldron), that is under the wooden fork from which cauldrons were suspended, as a sign of subordination, which is likely to have been a recognised symbolic practice.

Preiddeu Annwfn

I praise the lord, ruler of a king's realm
Who has extended his dominion over the shore of the world.
Well prepared was Gweir's prison in Caer Sidi
During the time of Pwyll and Pryderi.
No one went there before him.
The heavy blue grey chain held the faithful servant,
And before the spoils of Annwfn he sings in woe,
And our bardic invocation shall continue until doom.
Three times the fill of Prydwen we went into it;
Except seven, none returned from Caer Sidi.

I am fair in fame if my song is heard
In Caer Pedryfan, with its four sides revolving;
My poetry from the cauldron was uttered,
Ignited by the breath of nine maidens.
The cauldron of the chief of Annwfn, was sought
With its dark rim and pearls.
It does not boil the coward's portion, it is not its destiny.
A shining sword was thrust into it,
And it was left behind in Lleminog's hand.
And before the door of hell's gate, lamps burned.
And when we went with Arthur, glorious in misfortune,
Except seven, none returned from Caer Vedwyd.

I am fair in fame: my songs are heard
In Caer Pedryfan, Isle of the strong shining door
Fresh water and jet run together;
Bright wine their drink before their retinue.
Three times the fill of Prydwen we went by sea:
Except seven, none returned from Caer Rigor.

I set no value on insignificant men concerned with scripture,
They did not see the valour of Arthur beyond Caer Wydyr:
Six thousand men stood upon the wall.
It was hard to speak with their sentinel.
Three times the fill of Prydwen went with Arthur
Except seven, none returned from Caer Golud.

I set no value on insignificant men with their trailing robes
They do not know what was created on what day.
When at mid-day Cwy was born.
Or who made the one who did not go to the meadows of
    Defwy;
They do not know the Brindled ox or his yoke

With seven score links on his collar.
And when we went with Arthur, dolorous journey
Except seven none returned from Caer Vandwy.

I set no value on insignificant men with weak wills,
Who do not know on what day the chief was created,
When at mid-day the ruler was born,
What animal they keep with his silver head.
When we went with Arthur, piteous battle
Except seven none returned from Caer Ochren.

Congregating monks howl like a choir of dogs
From a clash with the lords who know
Whether the wind has one course, whether the sea is all one,
Whether the fire is all one spark of fierce tumult?

Monks congregate like wolves
From a clash with lords who know.
The monks do not know how the light and dark divide,
Nor the winds course, or the storm,
The place where it ravages, the place it strikes,
How many saints are in the Otherworld, how many on earth?
I praise the lord, the great chief:
May I not endure sadness: Christ will reward me.[10]

Cauldron of Goibniu / Cauldron of the Dagda

Also in Ireland, the cauldron belonging to the smith god, Goibniu, was used to prepare all the feasts of the Irish gods, the *Tuatha De*, and their chief god, the Dagda (The Good God, the all father) also had a famous cauldron of plenty. The Dagdha also had a club which would kill the living and resurrect the dead, much like the cauldron of Brân, the *pair dadeni*[11]. Again, we see the link between life and death and the switching between the two.

There is a final 'cauldron' of death and rebirth in Irish myth – that of the well of healing, Slainge's Well, (Old Irish: Tiprait Slainge) where the healer god, and son of the Dagda, Dian Cécht placed fallen warriors during the Second Battle of Magh Tuireadh (Cath Maige Tuired)[12]. While this is a well, rather than a cauldron, they share a great deal functionally and symbolically, and this well bears a striking resemblance to the *pair dadeni* in its role of resurrecting warriors. Here we see another trace of earlier tradition and belief, possibly threads of the same mythology and cult practice.

Endnotes

1   Julius Caesar, *The Gallic Wars* (Latin and English): *De Bello Gallico*, XIV. W. A. Macdevitt (Trans). neptunepublishing. us. Kindle Edition. neptunepublishing.us. 2018. Kindle Edition. Location 7016.

2   P. K. Ford. 1992. P 4.

3   L. Thorp, *Giraldus Cambrensis*, 2004. Location 3409.

4   S. Davies, trans. *The Mabinogion*, Oxford World Classics, Oxford University Press, 2007. p 54.

5   J. Mackillop. *Oxford dictionary of Celtic Mythology*, Oxford University Press, 1998. P 262.

6.   J.P. Clancy (trans) 'The Gododdin', *Medieval Welsh Poems,* Four Courts Press, 2003. P56.

7   M. Haycock, 2015. p174.

8   W. Y. Evans-Wentz, *The Fairy Faith in Celtic Countries*, Dover Publications, 2002, p157.

9   Bedd Taliesin. https://coflein.gov.uk/en/site/303607

10   D. Forest, *Gwyn ap Nudd - Wild God of Faerie, Guardian of Annwfn*, 2017. p 13-15. Note that my translation whilst aiming to be as accurate as possible comes from a bardic as well as a linguistic perspective. For more academic translations see Haycock, M. *Legendary poems from the book*

of Taliesin 2015, and Koch, J. 2003, '*The Heroic Age: Literary sources for ancient Celtic Europe and early Ireland and Wales.*' and Higley, S. Camelot Project, 2007, http://d.lib.rochester. edu/camelot/text/preiddeu-annwn. (Accessed 30/6/17)

11 S. Davies, 2007. p. 233.

12 J. Koch, 2006, p360.

Part 4

Connecting with Cerridwen

Invoking Cerridwen

There will be times in your practice where you will want to deepen and explore your own relationship with Cerridwen. For this reason, it will be necessary to begin invoking Cerridwen, and letting your own relationship with her guide and inspire you.

Invoking a deity – if that's what you think Cerridwen is, or any great and powerful spirit, takes a clarity of purpose and some dedication if it is to build a relationship that will grow and develop over time. Some people may feel instantly connected to her, and that is a wonderful thing, while others may feel disheartened if they do not feel a connection or response immediately, or if they do not feel called specifically by her, even though they would like to be. This happens regarding all kinds of gods and goddesses, where it may appear there is a hierarchy between those who feel called by a specific being, and those who would like a connection and have not yet. However, such comparisons between people, while human nature, are not really helpful to anyone and aren't indicative of anyone's relationship or closeness to their gods at all. We are all different and the gods have their own plans for us – just as we in our immortal selves, have our own plans for us too – we are not excluded if we feel we would like a connection but haven't felt singled out by Cerridwen, or any other god / being in the Celtic traditions. There is no knowing if one person's personal gnosis is more genuine or powerful than another's; some may feel called but be in error listening only to their desires, while others may feel a lack of a call due to their humility and self-doubt. Do not be overly put off or overly encouraged by anyone else's relationship with Cerridwen (or any other Celtic divinity) – your path is yours alone. Instead try to cultivate feeling present and enquiring, so that you gradually improve your sense of what it is you experience and what is your inner dialogue – develop the discernment to see how your inner self relates to the wider universe and the spirit realm, or Annwfn. This work on your self takes lifetimes and is perhaps endless, but is the most rewarding. That way when you meet your gods you can stand tall and as fully yourself as you can manage. The dialogue that may ensue is where the real spiritual riches can be found.

To call on Cerridwen, I would encourage setting some time aside every day, at least for a while and especially before any creative endeavour. I also encourage you to have a physical space set aside in your home, to use as an altar to her. This can be a wonderfully ornate feature in your home, or something as simple as a safe place to position a pilar candle which you light in her honour. An altar could include pictures of art inspired by Cerridwen, or passages from the poems of Taliesin printed out in an attractive way. It could also include flowers or a plant, special stones or objects that feel relevant to you, perhaps an incense burner or a bowl to place offerings. I have a small cauldron in which I can place a lit tea light or burn some incense which I place by my writing desk, but I also have a large pillar candle devoted to her and pieces or artwork devoted to her at my main altar, and a large print of Cerridwen by the artist Dan Goodfellow – the cover art of this book – in pride of place.

Whatever works for you, at least try getting yourself a large pillar candle, which you can light regularly and snuff out safely after each time you have worked with her. This way you have something that lasts beyond just one session, and takes time to be fully consumed, helping the relationship with her, and how you relate to her, to be something that develops over time and has some consistency. Some people may choose a specific colour to relate to her, green candles are popular for Cerridwen, as are yellow ones which relate to the element of air, for her inspiration. Others like to focus on her qualities as initiator, and see her as a 'crone goddess' although the Wiccan model of maiden mother and crone is not found in the Welsh or other Celtic traditions – none the less if this aspect of Cerridwen attracts you most a black candle may be suitable. I prefer a white or natural beeswax candle, and for me the quality of the candle is more important than the colour as I may call on all her various aspects at different times. There is no fixed way to invoke Cerridwen, and certainly no colour or other 'correspondences' that go with working with her other than those who come to people via their own experience and gnosis, so go with what feels right to you and allow yourself to experiment and adapt over time.

Invoking Cerridwen Candle Prayer

Take your candle, and see that you have a safe dedicated place where you can light it regularly until it is burned down and you replace it. You may like to anoint your candle with scented oil or herbs. I like to make my own oil with mugwort (recipe will be included in the herbs section) to call and strengthen my inner vision – and I use this to anoint my Cerridwen candle, perhaps placing a circle of dried mugwort and flowers around the candles base in a circle – not because this is ancient practice, but because I like to make her an offering in this way. Sometimes the flowers will be dried rose petals, or lavender, sometimes oak leaves or mistletoe, hazelnuts or whatever I feel drawn to use at the time.

Whenever I do a specific working spell, inner journey or prayer to Cerridwen, I light the candle with a fresh match, and invoke her assistance. Try these words or use you own as you feel:

Cerridwen, keeper of the cauldron of inspiration, I call to you for your guidance and power
Bless my work here.

I also like to use a section from one of Taliesin's poems which feels very fitting as an invocation, to call in her Awen...

Yr Awen a Ganaf, Or Dwfn y Dygaf
('I sing of the Awen, I draw it from the deep...')[1]

I chant and sing this nine times, three for land, three for sea, three for sky, as a simple charm to raise my power and my own Awen for the work. You could chant or say this in Welsh or in English if you prefer, although I encourage you to try it in Welsh, perhaps alternating even which language you use until it feels natural to you.

Spend some time gazing into the flame and enter into a gentle, meditative space, letting yourself reach out to Cerridwen seeking communion and inner vision. Let yourself just be quiet with her for a while and see what comes to you. Pay attention to how you feel in your body and any ideas or symbols which may flash into your mind.

After a while, thank Cerridwen for her assistance, and either proceed with one of the exercises listed in this book, or continue on with your own magic or creative endeavour.

When you are ready, bid her farewell with respect and reverence, using your own words, and snuff out the candle, before closing any sacred space or circle you may have created. Be sure that you are grounded afterwards and perhaps record any experiences in a journal.

A Cauldron Initiation

In this journey we will explore working with Cerridwen's cauldron for vision and insight. Use as a next step after the exercises working though the tale of Taliesin to take the process deeper.

First create a sacred space in whatever way feels right for you, and settle yourself comfortably. Traditionally those seeking Otherworld inspiration would sit in a darkened place, without any sensory information, and a stone upon their belly, in a sense placing them under the earth. If you feel to, I recommend this as a simple but very powerful practice. A rounded stone from a beach or river bed is best. You can arrange to do this worked in a darkened room away from any noise, or using the sound recording of a river to act as a block to any noise outside, or if you are able, you could even do this out in nature – in a remote spot or at a burial cairn if you can do so safely.

Remember when we seek wisdom in our inner vision, whether we use 'shamanic' style journeying, seership or simple guided visualisation, depends very much on our ability and experience as well as our state of mind at the time. We each of us have the capacity to engage with spirit and with our ancestral wisdom, but each of us will also do so according to our own capacity, and what one will see may not be the vision of another. For this reason, this exercise is designed to give you signposts along the way, but to allow you to have your own experience.

Focus on creating a sacred space that you are comfortable with, and will be uninterrupted in for an extended period of time, perhaps an hour or more, and take three deep slow breaths down into your belly, for earth, another three for sea, and anther three for sky.

Ask aloud that Cerridwen bless your visions and insights here today, and grant you the gift of Awen.

See yourself walking along a pale stone path, downhill towards a vast lake, which shines a deep blue, reflecting the night sky above it clear and crisp as a mirror.

As you walk, remember and honour the changes you have undertaken in studying Cerridwen's tale an say to yourself and to Her,

> *I have been a hare and a hound, I have been a salmon and an otter, a bird and a hawk, I have sat in the womb of Cerridwen, and been cast upon the sea...*

As you walk you see the flicker of flames ahead of you, where Cerridwen awaits, the bubbling cauldron beside her, sending great plumes of steam, spiralling up into the sky.

Great her as mistress of the mysteries, as initiatrix. What wisdom does she have for you at this time? If you wish you may ask her for a glimpse into her cauldron, and bowing your head, peer into its depth for a while. You must not tell another what you see.

Cerridwen may offer you a sip of her brew or she may decide that more time and work are needed. Follow and respect her guidance at this time in all things.

Here at the shore of the lake, with the goddess before you, when the time is right, repeat the lines

> *Yr Awen a Ganaf, Or Dwfn y Dygaf*
> ('I sing of the Awen, I draw it from the depths...')

slowly like a mantra, learning the words by heart... at this deeper invocation Cerridwen may show you visions, either in this exercise or within your dreams at a later date.

Complete your time with Cerridwen by showing your devotion, intoning the Awen nine times, saying aloud 'ah-oo-ennn' slowly and with care – controlling your breath and paying attention to pitch and rhythm. There is no right or wrong way to do this, but seek to use your voice as a method of magic making, or of devotion and prayer, as a vehicle for the Awen, the divine breath – to come through you into the world. Experiment and be creative!

When you are ready, thank Cerridwen, and return the way you came, using your breath to draw yourself back into your body, from your chest and expanding back into the everyday world, before wiggling your fingers and toes and feeling yourself fully back in the room. As always, you may like to record your experiences in a journal.

Pilgrimages and Vigils

In addition to these journeys and invocations, I encourage you to spend time out in nature to develop your Awen and your connection to Cerridwen – seek quiet places, mountains and lakesides, and if you can, to visit the areas mentioned in her tale – Snowdonia and Bala in particular.

Take time getting to know the quieter wilder places, spend time gazing into open fires, and listening to the sound of the river and the wind in the trees – these are all things that will build your Awen and help you hear and heed the wisdom of the Otherworld.

Seek time each day to honour Cerridwen, and notice the liminal places and times, in your day and in your life – dawn and dusk, the turn of the seasons, the moments before your life changes, beginnings and endings, and consider how Cerridwen may help you to access that which lies beyond, beyond space and time, between and beyond our mortal lives, and remember such wisdom is only, ever a hare's (and hound's) breath away.

Endnote

1   Taliesin, 'Angar Kyfundawt', (The Malign Confederacy), translated by D. Forest, 2023. For an academic translation see Marged Haycock, *Legendary poems from the book of Taliesin*, CMCS, 2015. p119.

Conclusion

Cerridwen, keeper of the cauldron, oversees many aspects of the Welsh and Brythonic mysteries – mistress of magic and inspiration, she holds and controls access to the Otherworld via her potent and mysterious brew. By treading the paths of those who came before us, and learning what traces of tradition are left to us in the remaining lore, we may draw closer to her, deepen our knowledge, and catch a glimpse of her as she has been in the past, aligning with her currents and knowing her not only by the face she shows the world now, as a goddess of magic, but also as she was known long ago; one who knew the mysteries of life and death and all that lies beyond. Her older faces, and older names, may be lost or at least now largely forgotten, but still she stands, calling to us on the wind from the Otherworld, to come to the edge of things, look into her cauldron, and be changed forever by what we see.

May we be blessed by the vision!

Bendithion!

Appendix 1

A Cerridwen Herbal

There are no herbs specifically related to Cerridwen from the traditional lore, however, there are several useful herbs found in Britian and Wales specifically that could be relevant and useful for your work with Her. Herbs have always been used for their healing, protective, magical and spiritual effects within the Celtic traditions. The subject is too huge to fully cover here but below is a selection of a few which can provide an introduction and can be used as offerings and to support your personal connection and inner vision, and which I have found useful in my practice. Feel free to add to this list using your own intuition, but always also base your practice with herbs on traditional and medicinal lore where available as herbs can be dangerous if not used wisely. Always buy dried herbs from an ethical supplier.

Always consult a Medicinal herbalist before ingesting any herbs for healing purposes especially if you have any health conditions.

Common Mugwort – *Artemisia vulgaris*
Traditionally sacred to the moon, Mugwort can be found growing wild across the British Isles – it prefers rough areas with good sunlight but grows in many environments. It can also be bought dried online. Mugwort is used for protection and for increasing the inner vision – mugwort tea is useful for dream work and gives powerfully prophetic dreams and increases intuition. It is also used in incense or burned as a herb bundle to clear a space of negative energies and to consecrate an area as sacred for spiritual use such as meditation. Cold mugwort tea

is also used to ritually cleanse magical tools. Mugwort oil can be used to anoint the brow for vision seeking and for anointing ritual candles.

Mugwort is sometimes used to help regulate the menstrual cycle but it can seriously increase heavy bleeding. Use with extreme caution if you are experiencing heavy periods and avoid ingesting or breathing it in if you are pregnant. Also do not use mugwort if breastfeeding.

Mugwort as incense – the dried herb can be burned on charcoal incense bricks or as a herb bundle rather like a Native American smudge stick. In Gaelic Scotland this is called Saining – to sanctify.

Mugwort herb sachet – place dried mugwort in a small cloth pouch placed under the pillow for prophetic dreams and protection.

Mugwort tea – one teaspoon of dried mugwort per mug of hot water – steep for 10 minutes.

Mugwort oil – half fill a glass jar with dried or fresh mugwort and fill the jar with olive or sunflower oil. Leave in a sunny window for one month before straining, decanting into a fresh jar and storing in a dark cool cupboard. This will keep for around a year.

Rowan – *Sorbus aucuparia*

Rowan is a highly protective tree, and rowan wood and berries are both used in Celtic practice to ward off ill intentions, and to help the practitioner see what issues or dangers may surround them – awareness providing the best protection of all. Rowan can be found across Europe and North America.

A small stick of rowan wood can be tied with red thread and hung by doors and windows or placed under pillows for protection – they were traditionally placed under babies' cribs to protect from faeries as well as to protect livestock.

Rowan berries can be threaded into necklaces and bracelets to grant the wearer protection and increase magical vision. Wood of the rowan can be burnt in ritual fires. Rowan berry oil can be used to anoint the body or ritual items.

Rowan berry oil – gather fresh or dried rowan berries and half fill a glass jar – filling the remainder of the jar with olive or sunflower oil, leave on a sunny windowsill for one month before storing in a dark cool cupboard. There is no need to strain the oil unless you wish to. This should keep for around a year.

Vervain – *Verbena officinalis*

Vervain was one of the most sacred herbs of the druids where it is used to create sacred spaces and is traditionally said to open the avenues of communication between the practitioner and the spirit realm. Medicinally it is a nervine and is good for relaxing the mind, making it a good addition to working with Cerridwen and seeking the Awen. It grows wild in many places throughout the British Isles and can also be bought from herbal garden centres – dried vervain is available from most herbal suppliers. Vervain can be burnt or given as an offering or in incense, drunk as a herbal tea, or used in herbal charm bags.

Vervain tea – one teaspoon of dried vervain in one mug of boiling water – steep for 10 minutes.

Vervain oil – half fill one jar with dried vervain, fill the rest of the jar with olive or sunflower oil, and leave on a sunny windowsill for one month before straining and storing in a dark cool space. This should keep for around a year.

Dried bunches of vervain can be hung around doors window and around magical altars to bless and consecrate them.

Meadowsweet – *Filipendula ulmaria*

Meadowsweet grows abundantly in wild places in Wales and across Britian, preferring damp ditches and waterways. Its frothy white flowers smell beautiful and it is used magically for love, blessing and bringing peace – it is a good offering to Cerridwen and can aid in divination and protection work. Hang bunches of meadowsweet to dry over your altar as an offering which can also be used when dried in incense and as a tea as well as in herbal charm bags – placed under the pillow it helps receive pleasant dreams.

A Charm Bag for Cerridwen

Carry or place under your pillow for closer connection to Cerridwen and to increase the intuition. Gather your herbs and dry them yourself if you can. Use equal parts mugwort, rowan, vervain and mugwort. Place your herbs in a small cloth pouch, thanking the spirit of each herb as you place it the bag. Tie it three times, asking the spirits of each plant to lend you their guidance and protection, to increase your inner vision and learn the ways of the Awen. Replace after three months.

A Cerridwen Vision Brew

Gather one teaspoon each of mugwort, vervain and mint or lemon balm for flavour, brewed in one large mug of boiling fresh or bottled spring water for 10 minutes, stirring clockwise continuously, whilst chanting the Awen. Leave to cool and add honey to taste. Drink before bed or before divination or meditative vision work.

Do not ingest mugwort if pregnant or breastfeeding or having menstrual issues without first consulting a medicinal herbalist.

A Cerridwen Incense

1 spoon of dried mugwort
1 spoon of crushed dried rowan berries
1 spoon of dried vervain
1 spoon of dried meadowsweet
1 spoon dried juniper berries

2–3 spoons of frankincense (obviously this isn't native to Wales, I just found I liked to add it in my practice, ethically sourced).

2–3 spoons of pine resin.

A Note on Mushrooms and Entheogens

It must be mentioned, that like almost everywhere in the world, Wales and Britain generally have their own naturally occurring wild entheogenic plants, the most famous of these are *Psilocybe semilanceata,* also known as magic mushrooms or liberty caps, and *Amanita Muscaria,* fly agaric. While debates have raged on this for years, it seems unlikely that in the Iron Age and later when country people would know all the plants growing in their area, and all their accompanying properties, such powerful plants and their effects could be over looked, but the fact is we have little evidence either way. That said, there are interesting designs on the Gundestrup cauldron that look tantalisingly like magic mushrooms, and their tendency to grow in wild places, especially the Welsh mountains naturally lead one to consider whether this would have been an ingredient in any initiatory brew used in bardic or other Welsh mystical traditions before the Christian era. Certainly, the search for inspiration and magical knowledge extended far beyond merely seeking poetic rhyme and metre, into encompassing a knowledge of all things, something those experiencing the effects of entheogens commonly describe. This is not in any way to recommend or endorse the use of these substances, about which we sadly now know considerably less than we once did, reducing how safely and legally we can use them. However, it does seem that with the proper knowledge and support such plants could have played a central role in any initiation process within the Celtic lands, just as they do in other parts of the world, along with the host of herbs and other plants that are still available to us legally, that can also support the visionary journey, healing and health.

Appendix 2

Pronunciation Guide

Cerridwen – Ke-RID-wen
Taliesin – Tal-yes-in
Gwion – Gwee-onn
Awen – ow-wen
Awenyddion- ow-wen-uth-yon
Llyn Tegid – hlin- teg-id
Ceredigion – ker-eh-DIG-yon
Bendithion – Ben-dith-yon
Annwfn – ann-O-vn
Aerwen – ire-wenn
Creirwy – Cray -oey
Tegid Foel – Teg-id-voil
Morda – Morr-daa
Morfran – mor-vran
Afagddu – a-vag-thee

'Yr Awen a Ganaf, Or Dwfn y Dygaf' – er-ow-wen-a-gan-av, or dovn-uh-dee-gav

Bibliography

S. Baring-Gould, and J. Fisher, *The Lives of the British Saints: The Saints of Wales and Cornwall and Such Irish Saints as Have Dedications in Britain, Volume 2*, C. J. Clark, 1908.

R. Bromwich, *Trioedd Ynys Prydein: The Triads of the Island of Britain*, University of Wales Press, Cardiff, 2017.

J.P. Clancy, (trans) *'The Gododdin'*, *Medieval Welsh Poems*, Four Courts Press, 2003.

E. Davies, *The Mythology and Rites of the British Druids*, J. Booth, London, 1909.

S. Davies, trans. *The Mabinogion*, Oxford World Classics, Oxford University Press, 2007.

W. Y. Evans-Wentz, *The Fairy Faith in Celtic Countries*, Dover Publications, 2002, p157.

P. K. Ford, *Ystoria Taliesin*, University of Wales Press, Cardiff, 1992.

D. Forest, *Gwyn ap Nudd – Wild God of Faerie, Guardian of Annwfn*, Moon Books, 2017.

I. L. Foster, *'Gwynn ap Nudd'*, in *Duanaire Finn*, iii, ed. Gerard Murphy, Irish Texts Society, no. 43 (Dublin, 1953).

M. Haycock, *Legendary poems from the book of Taliesin*, CMCS, 2015.

R. Hutton, *The Pagan Religions of the Ancient British Isles: Their Nature and Legacy*, Blackwell Publishing, 1993.

J. Koch, *Celtic Culture - A Historical Encyclopaedia*, A B C C L I O, 2006.

J. Koch, J. Carey, *The Celtic Heroic Age. Celtic Studies Publications*, Aberystwyth, 2003.

W. A. Macdevitt, (trans) *Julius Caesar, The Gallic Wars (Latin and English): De Bello Gallico*, XIV. neptunepublishing.us. Kindle Edition. neptunepublishing.us. 2018. Kindle Edition. Location 7016.

J. Mackillop, *Oxford dictionary of Celtic Mythology*, Oxford University Press, 1998.

Nennius, *History of the Britons (Historia Brittonum)*, (trans, J.A. Giles, Project Gutenberg, 1972) Kindle edition.

R. Pitcairn, *Ancient Criminal Trials in Scotland, vol. 3, part 2*, Bannatyne Club, 1883.

J. Rowland, *Early Welsh Saga Poetry: A study and Edition of the Englynion*, D.S. Brewer, 1990.

L. Thorpe, (trans) *Gerald of Wales, The Journey through Wales and the Description of Wales*, Kindle edition, Penguin classics 2004.

I. Williams, *Chwedl Taliesin*, University of Wales, Board of Celtic Studies, Cardiff. 1957.

You may also like

PAGAN PORTALS
ĠWYN
AP NUDD
WILD GOD OF FAERIE
GUARDIAN OF ANNWFN

DANU FOREST

978-1-78535-629-2 (Paperback)
978-1-78535-630-8 (e-book)

Readers of ebooks can buy or view any of these bestsellers by clicking on the live link in the title. Most titles are published in paperback and as an ebook. Paperbacks are available in traditional bookshops. Both print and ebook formats are available online.

Find more titles and sign up to our readers' newsletter
www.collectiveinkbooks.com/paganism

For video content, author interviews and more, please subscribe to our YouTube channel.

MoonBooksPublishing

Follow us on social media for book news, promotions and more:

Facebook: Moon Books

Instagram: @MoonBooksCI

Twitter: @MoonBooksCI

TikTok: @MoonBooksCI